KENDO

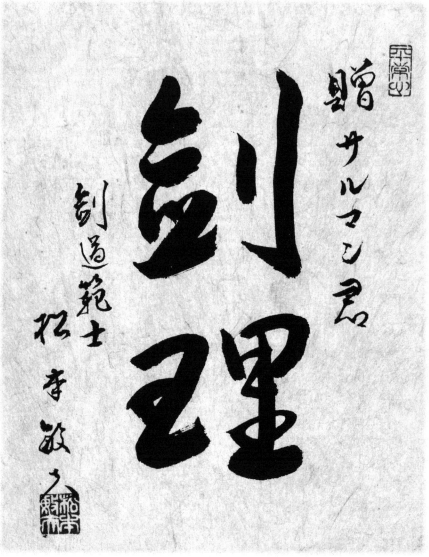

Kenri—Calligraphy by Matsumoto Toshio Hanshi 9th Dan. The kanji shown here and on the front cover can be read as "Sword Theory," although they also convey a spectrum of deeper meaning to experienced kenshi.

KENDO

A COMPREHENSIVE GUIDE TO JAPANESE SWORDSMANSHIP

GEOFF SALMON

with illustrations by
KATSUYA MASAGAKI

TUTTLE Publishing

Tokyo   Rutland, Vermont │ Singapore

"Books to Span the East and West"

Tuttle Publishing was founded in 1832 in the small New England town of Rutland, Vermont [USA]. Our core values remain as strong today as they were then—to publish best-in-class books which bring people together one page at a time. In 1948, we established a publishing outpost in Japan—and Tuttle is now a leader in publishing English-language books about the arts, languages and cultures of Asia. The world has become a much smaller place today and Asia's economic and cultural influence has grown. Yet the need for meaningful dialogue and information about this diverse region has never been greater. Over the past seven decades, Tuttle has published thousands of books on subjects ranging from martial arts and paper crafts to language learning and literature—and our talented authors, illustrators, designers and photographers have won many prestigious awards. We welcome you to explore the wealth of information available on Asia at www.tuttlepublishing.com.

Published by Tuttle Publishing, an imprint of Periplus Editions (HK) Ltd.

www.tuttlepublishing.com

Copyright © 2013 Geoff Salmon

Library of Congress Catalog # 2013016558

ISBN 978-4-8053-1231-5

Distributed by

North America, Latin America & Europe
Tuttle Publishing
364 Innovation Drive,
North Clarendon, VT 05759-9436 U.S.A.
Tel: 1 (802) 773-8930; Fax: 1 (802) 773-6993
info@tuttlepublishing.com
www.tuttlepublishing.com

Japan
Tuttle Publishing
Yaekari Building, 3rd Floor, 5-4-12 Osaki
Shinagawa-ku, Tokyo 141 0032
Tel: (81) 3 5437-0171; Fax: (81) 3 5437-0755
sales@tuttle.co.jp
www.tuttle.co.jp

Asia Pacific
Berkeley Books Pte. Ltd.
3 Kallang Sector #04-01, Singapore 349278
Tel: (65) 6741-2178; Fax: (65) 6741-2179
inquiries@periplus.com.sg
www.tuttlepublishing.com

First edition
26 25 24 23   11 10 9 8 7   2307CM
Printed in China

TUTTLE PUBLISHING® is a registered trademark of Tuttle Publishing, a division of Periplus Editions (HK) Ltd.

Contents

CHAPTER 1

Introduction......................7
The Purpose of Kendo................ 9
Kendo for Life............................ 10
Equipment and how to choose
   and wear it 12
Reigi.. 27
   Posture and Kamae................... 34
   Maai.. 39
   Footwork 42
   Breathing and Kiai................... 44
   Metsuke................................... 45
   Yuko-Datotsu 46

CHAPTER 2

Waza **51**
   Mitsu no sen 51

Shikake Waza.......................**52**
   Sutemi.................................... 52
   Men-uchi................................ 53
   Kote-uchi................................ 56
   Dou uchi................................. 59
   Gyaku-dou 61
   Tsuki 62
   Timing and opportunity for
     shikake waza 64

Tobikomi waza........................ 64
Hikibana waza......................... 64
Debana waza 65
Harai waza............................... 69
Osae waza................................ 71
Uchiotoshi............................... 72
Makiotoshi and Makiage.......... 73
Renzoku waza 73
Hiki Waza................................ 76
Seme, tame, and the Four
   Sicknesses 80
Sansappo or Sansatsuho........... 81

CHAPTER 3

Oji waza..**82**
   Men nuki men 82
   Kote nuki men 84
   Kote nuki kote......................... 85
   Men nuki dou 86
   Men suriage men...................... 87
   Tsuki suriage men.................... 89
   Kote suriage men 90
   Kote suriage kote 91
   Men kaeshi dou 92
   Men kaeshi men....................... 94
   Kote kaeshi kote....................... 96

Dou uchiotoshi men 98

Tsuki nayashi tsuki 99

Footwork for oji waza 100

CHAPTER 4

Kendo Training Methods 101

Kihon Geiko 101

Motodachi geiko and mawari geiko 102

Motodachi 103

Kirikaeshi 105

Uchikomi geiko 108

Kakarigeiko 110

Butsukarigeiko 111

Yakusoku Geiko 111

Waza geiko **112**

Shikake waza geiko 112

Oji waza geiko 124

Jigeiko 143

Kata geiko 147

CHAPTER 5

Structuring a kendo session **151**

Other structures 152

Warm up and cool down exercises 153

Hitori geiko 161

Practicing with children 172

Other forms of training 173

Shiai 175

Refereeing Kendo Matches 178

Grading Examinations 181

Glossary/Index **184**

CHAPTER 1

Introduction

This book is written expressly with the objective of helping you make your kendo training more effective. It is aimed both at people starting to climb the kendo ladder and more advanced students who want to ensure they are making the most of their time in the dojo. Without attempting to delve into kendo's lineage and history, I have peppered this book with elements of its philosophy—simply because you cannot divorce physical actions from the reasons for doing them. Whether your objective for practicing kendo is to train your mind to achieve a state of *mushin* (no-mind), or be a winner in competition—or simply to keep fit—it helps to know why things are done a certain way.

I do not claim to have invented a secret formula for success. All the ideas here are "out there" and have repeatedly been impressed on me by a number of senior teachers over my forty-plus-year kendo career. There are no short cuts in kendo, but there are ways to ensure that you do not waste time doing things that are useless or counterproductive. When I started kendo in the UK in the early 1970s, we were pretty much cut off from the pool of knowledge that existed in Japan. Despite the efforts of one or two pioneers who knew more than the rest of us, a lot of technique was self-taught. I went on to live and work in Japan where I had access to some of the great second generation sensei. I did however, have to spend my first year unlearning my bad habits and starting again from scratch. Clearly the most effective way to improve is to start by doing things correctly and to conscientiously continue the correct practice of basic techniques throughout your kendo career.

This or any other guide is in no way a substitute for a good instructor. While we now have access to print and online resources from some of the world's best kendoka, it is important to train with a teacher who can monitor your progress and make suggestions that are relevant to you. Your choice of instructor will have a major effect on your progress, so do put some thought into your selection. If you live in a major city, then you will probably have a choice of dojo. Go and watch some sessions before committing to join. Not all technically skilled kendoka are good teachers and vice versa. It is also worth talking to other members of the class.

If there is not a choice of dojo in your area, you need to make the best of what is available. In some cases you may have to work with a junior instructor or even train with your peers, taking turns to lead the practice. My only word of caution is that in these cases everyone should be aware of their own ability level and seek opportunities to attend seminars and club visits and invite senior instructors to visit whenever you can. In this way you get exposure to new ideas and can all improve together. I have seen a few rare cases where an inexperienced club instructor has forbidden students to train with other teachers. This is perhaps forgivable of very highly ranked teachers if students are going through the basics stage, but coming from lesser kendoka this smacks of conceit and cultism.

As a last resort you can train alone. I have included a section on hitori geiko, however these exercises should ideally to be practiced in addition to the work you do in the dojo. Kendo is a social and sociable art and is best done with others.

Readers' note

International Kendo uses Japanese terminology extensively to describe equipment, techniques, and training methodology. I have therefore used this Japanese labeling throughout the book. In most cases I have done so without the customary italics. In line with Japanese grammar rules on compound words, I have made some consonant changes, so for instance kote becomes gote and futon becomes buton.

The Purpose of Kendo

In 1975 the All Japan Kendo Federation (AJKF) developed and published "The Concept and Purpose of Kendo" which is reproduced below.

Concept

"Kendo is a way to discipline the human character through the application of the principles of the katana."

Purpose

To mold the mind and body.
To cultivate a vigorous spirit,
And through correct and rigid training,
To strive for improvement in the art of Kendo.
To hold in esteem human courtesy and honor.
To associate with others with sincerity.
And to forever pursue the cultivation of oneself.
Thus will one be able:
To love one's country and society;
To contribute to the development of culture;
And to promote peace and prosperity among all peoples

Kendo for Life

Kendo is unusual in that it allows the generations to train together. Children from five upwards can enjoy kendo practice. At the other end of the scale it is possible to continue to enjoy keiko at an age when most other martial artists have hung up their boots or donated their dogi to the charity shop. Numerous sensei continue not only to be great teachers, but also remain formidable opponents into their 70s and 80s.

To quote the famous Taisho period 10th dan, Mochida Seiji sensei:

Until you are 50 years old, you must endeavor to practice the fundamentals of kendo and make it a part of you. It has taken me 50 years to learn the fundamentals of kendo by body. It was not until I became 50 years old that I started my true kendo training. This is because I practiced kendo with all my heart and spirit.

When one becomes 60 years old, the legs are not as strong as they once were. It is the spirit that overcomes this weakness. It is through a strong spirit that one can overcome the inevitability of the body becoming physically weaker.

When I became 70 years old, the entire body became weaker. I found that the next step is to practice the concept of not moving one's spirit when practicing kendo. When one is able to achieve the state of an

Cross generation Kendo—the late Oshima Hideharu Sensei with his grandson

immovable spirit, your opponent's spirit will manifest itself to you. I tried to achieve a calm and immovable spirit at this stage in my life.

When I became 80 years old, I achieved the state of the immovable spirit. However, there are times when a random thought will enter my mind. I am striving to eliminate these random thoughts.

Very few of us will come close to Mochida sensei's level of accomplishment, but we can take comfort in the fact that kendo does not need to be abandoned as we get into our later years. In fact for many kendoka, their kendo career really takes off after retirement.

For people who take up kendo after they reach 50, it is still possible to advance into the higher dan ranks. A sensible approach to how hard and how fast you train is essential, as is correct warm-up and cool-down exercise. Nevertheless, good strong technique can be developed that works against younger, faster opponents and if you can come anywhere close to developing Mochida sensei's state of "the immovable spirit" or Fudoshin you become invincible.

Fudō Myō-ō, the Buddhist guardian deity that personifies Fudōshin

Equipment and How to Choose and Wear it

Kendo requires more equipment than many other sports. Over basic clothing of hakama and keikogi we wear bogu (armor), consisting of men, dou, tare, and kote. In addition we need at least one shinai (bamboo sword) and a tenugui (men towel).

Chakuso

Chakuso or the way we put on our equipment and present ourselves in kendo is an important indicator of our attitude to training and our technical ability. Bogu is expensive, so there is no problem in using old, well worn equipment. It should, however, be kept in good repair. Hakama and keikogi should be clean and pressed and wherever possible should retain the original color. I was given a lesson on the importance of good chakuso as well as one on Japanese tact early in my time in Osaka. My dojo's shihan explained that the cut-down judo jacket I used had been "stolen" and that I would have to wear the purpose made keikogi that he gave by way of "consolation."

Keikogi

Keikogi is the kendo jacket, a thick kimono style garment. Most people wear blue (indigo or synthetic indigo dyed) keikogi, although white is also

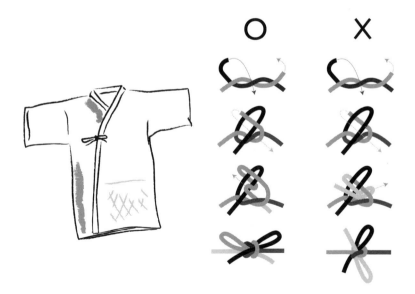

common. The original reason for using indigo as a dye was because of its antiseptic qualities should the wearer be wounded. The color of the keikogi has no real significance, but children and women sometimes wear white. White is also the preferred color of The Imperial Palace Police. Keikogi come in a wide range of qualities and thicknesses, from thin summer weight to double thickness. Double thickness keikogi tend to last longer and give more protection against off target hits.

Keikogi are simple to put on, just ensure that you wrap from left to right and tie the munehimo in a horizontal bow. The keikogi should fit so that the collar does not show a gap at the nape of your neck and the back of the keikogi should be smoothed down so that it is free from wrinkles. Keikogi sizes vary from maker to maker, so it pays to take the advice of your equipment supplier. It may sometimes be necessary to move the munehimo, or tabs that hold the keikogi closed at the front, to ensure a close fit at the collar.

Hakama

Kendo hakama also come in blue or white. The hakama has five pleats at the front and one at the back. The five front pleats are said to represent the Gojo or five virtues Jin-Gi-Rei-Chi-Shin

Jin - Humanity
Gi - Truth and Justice
Rei - Courtesy
Chi - Wisdom
Shin – Faith

The pleat at the back of the hakama symbolises Makoto or sincerity.

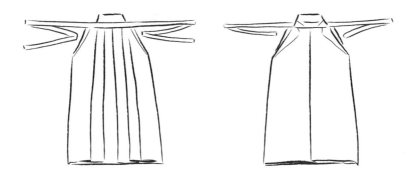

Hakama are available in tetron, polyester, or cotton. Cotton hakama are available in various weights designated by a thread density number ranging from 5,000 to 10,000. As a rule cotton is preferable to synthetic materials as it is absorbent and the weight makes it hang better. It is also wise to buy the heaviest quality cotton you can afford as it retains its pleats better. When you buy a hakama the pleats are normally tacked with cotton. It will never look as good again, but the cotton has to come out before you use it.

View from back

Putting on the hakama takes some getting used to. You should always put your left leg in first and take it out first when taking off the hakama. The only rationale I have heard for this is that if you are attacked, you can easily drop the hakama and move forward with your right leg.

When you have both legs in you should pull up the front of the hakama so that the top edge is just under your belly button. You then pass the long tapes from the front of the hakama around your waist and cross them under your abdomen at about six inches (15 cm) below the top edge of the hakama. As you do this, turn the tapes over so that they "lock" in place. Then keeping the tension on, take the tapes round to your back and tie in a bow. At this stage, pull your keikogi down so that it does not bunch up at the back. Once the front is in place, you should find a plastic tag on the inside of the hakama below the koshi -ita. Push this inside the bow and then take the rear tapes and cross them over and take the top tape under the point where the front tapes cross. Tie a flat knot and tuck each tape over the tapes at the sides of the hakama, ensuring that they are pushed down tightly. When worn, the front of the hakama should come to just above your toes and be slightly higher at the back.

Both keikogi and hakama should be folded after practice as per the diagrams. Before first use they should be soaked in cool water with the addition of either a cup of salt or white vinegar to help set the indigo dye. Even when this is done they will continue to bleed color, so they should be washed separately by hand in cool water. A useful tip to keep in mind is that if you pull them into shape immediately after washing and hang them in sunlight it will minimise the need for ironing. You should hang the keikogi inside out to avoid sun bleaching and use a clip type hanger to keep the hakama's pleats in place.

How to fold a hakama

First straighten the back pleat and then turn over to ensure that the front pleats are in place. Fold in the outside edges so that the hakama forms a rectangle. Make two even folds, taking the hakama to a third of its length. Now double up each of the long rear obi ties to form an even X shape the size of the folded hakama. Take the two short front obi ties over and under the center of the X and loop over the ties nearest to you. Finally secure by pulling the loose end on the left through the top right loop.

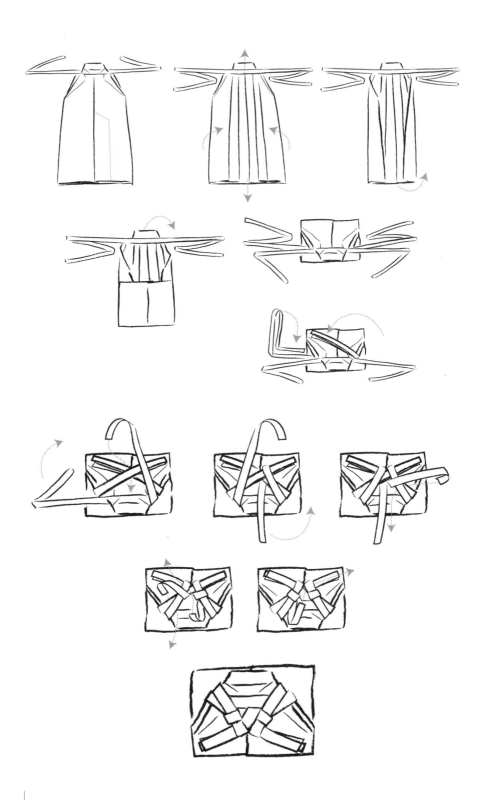

Folding Keikogi

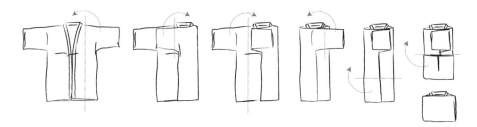

Bogu

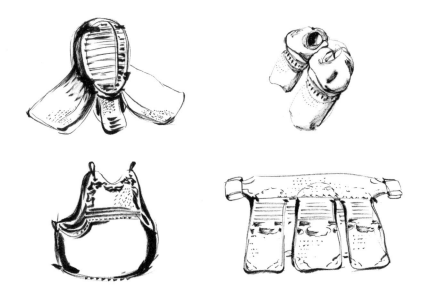

Selecting bogu or armor is even more baffling. The choice of styles, qualities, and brands is enormous as is the price range. You can buy hand-stitched, machine-stitched, even machine-stitched to look like hand-stitched bogu. Dou are available with traditional bamboo dou plates covered in leather and lacquer or made from synthetic material. So you need to think long and hard about what quality bogu you need and how much you are prepared to pay for it.

The two main types of bogu are hand-stitched and machine-stitched. The former is vastly more expensive and a top class handmade bogu may take several years to make and equates to the price of a new car. Both hand-stitched and machine-stitched armor is classified by the closeness of the stitching. Machine stitching normally comes in .24 inches (6mm), .16 inch (4mm) or

.12 inch (3mm) whereas hand stitching uses the traditional Japanese measures of bu and rin and ranges from 1bu through 1bu 2rin to 1bu 5rin to 2bu.

The more space between stitches the lower the price, so .24 inches (6mm) bogu is less expensive than .12 inch (3mm) and likewise 2bu is less expensive than 1bu. It is worth bearing in mind that loose stitched bogu needs to be thick, because it works by absorbing impact. Tight stitching deflects, so it is as much a case of personal preference as to which is best. A new type of 2bu hand-stitched armor is enjoying a boom at the moment as it is soft and light.

What you buy is up to you and your bank manager, but the only advice I would give you is to check what material goes into the construction of the bogu. Ideally it should be made from compressed wool felt and cotton, whereas some cheaper quality sets are padded with foam rubber which breaks down inside the covering and leaves the wearer more susceptible to injury. It is also essential to ensure that your bogu fits correctly, particularly your men and kote. Badly fitting bogu will be uncomfortable and make keiko more difficult. Your men should be a good fit for the size of your face and should be deep enough to finish level with the back of your head. Your eyes should line up with the space between the 6th and 7th bars from the top. Kote are made to fit your hand in the grip position so need not be measured against an open hand; instead they should fit comfortably when your hand is in grip position. Fingers should not be compressed and there should be no excess room in the atama or hand part of the kote. The protruding bones in the wrist itself should be protected by the kote buton "the main sleeve" and not the softer tsutsu.

Putting on bogu

Bogu should be put on sitting in seiza. First on is the tare which should line up with the top of the hakama. The tare obi should be passed around the waist and tied under the front flap. The dou follows with the longer himo taken over your back and crossed over the opposite shoulder. The himo should then be pushed through the chichikawa leather at the top of the dou and a loop made around the main part and the himo. The loop should lean towards the outside of the chichikawa and the remaining end should be pushed inside the dou. The other long himo should be tied in the same way, aiming to keep the dou level. Finally the short himo at the bottom of the dou should be tied across your back in a horizontal bow. The dou should sit just above the bottom of the tare waistband.

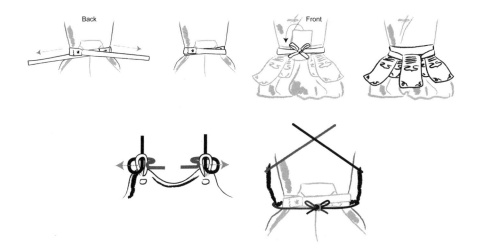

Dou and tare can be put on either in the dojo or the changing room depending on the dojo custom.

Placing men and kote

Men and kote are put on in the dojo at the command "Men wo tsuke." We will again touch on this when we look at reigi.

Your men and kote should be placed together by your right knee in line with those of the rest of the dojo members. Men himo should be folded neatly and placed inside the men. The positioning of kote and tenugui varies from dojo to dojo. Some favor the kote in a straight line from your body; others stipulate a 90 degree angle with the left kote in front. Some dojo drape fresh tenugui over the men; others keep it folded and place it inside.

Tying tenugui

There are various ways that the tenugui can be worn. Two require the tenugui to be tied as you put on your men. The other uses a clever origami technique to prefabricate a tenugui hat.

Method 1

Holding the two rear corners, pull the tenugui tightly against the back of your head bringing the left hand corner across to the right and cover the resultant flap by repeating the process from the right. You now have a triangular flap made up of the two tenugui ends in front of your eyes. Pull this straight back, tucking the tail end under if necessary, so that it does not protrude from the back of your men.

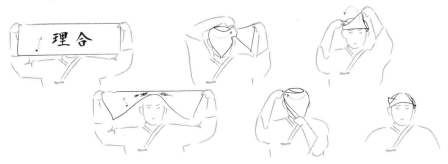

Method 2

Hold the center of the lower edge between your teeth. Pull the left and then the right edges of the tenugui around the back of your head and tie the two top corners in front of the top of your forehead. Release the lower edge and pull backwards.

Method 3

Double the tenugui lengthwise, fold ends in to form a triangle. Turn inside out and place on head. This is particularly useful for young children.

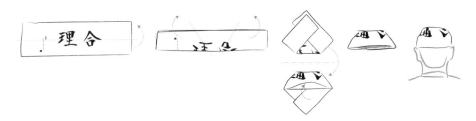

Tying Men Himo

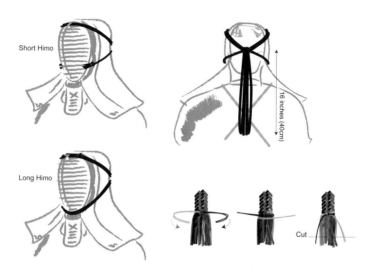

Here are two ways of tying a men, from the top with long "kansai himo" or from the bottom with shorter "kanto himo." The second method is simpler and more usual, so we will stick with this. The himo are tied at the fourth from bottom bar and pre-threaded through the top bars of the men and placed inside. After tying the tenugui we take out the ends of the men himo and hold them in our left hand while pulling open the himo which are already in place at the back of the men. Holding the men from the tsukidate, push your face in chin first. Pull both himo tight from the top then tie a half knot at the back, turning it into a bow which should sit in the groove at the base of your skull. You should ensure that the loops and tails of your men himo are of equal length and that they do not exceed 16 inches (40cm). For some obscure reason, even short himo are made a fraction too long to achieve this, so if you want to get it right, be prepared to get the scissors out. Kendo himo if cut will fray, so it is necessary to retie the ends as shown above.

Kote

With kote, the futon or wrist part should be laced tightly enough so that it does not move too much when it is hit, but it should also be loose enough to get your hand in easily. The futon should retain its tubular shape and not be allowed to open at the end like a cone. If laces are too long they should be cut, sealed at the end with vinyl tape, and retied as shown. The hands of the kote should be big enough for you to move your fingers comfortably and cover the whole of your palm.

Shinai

In modern kendo we use yotsuware shinai made from four strips of bamboo. These bamboo (*take*) are held together with a leather cap (sakigawa), a leather strip tied at a quarter of the shinai's length (nakayui), and a leather handle (tsukagawa). The leather fittings are held together by a tightly tied string (tsuru) which represents the back of the blade. Inside the shinai, a sakigomu supports the kissaki and a metal plate or chigiri the handle.

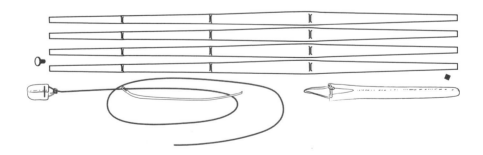

Shinai weights are regulated for competition as follows:

FIK Specifications for competition use of one Shinai (Itto).				
Specification	Gender	Junior High School (12–15 yrs)	Senior High School (15–18 yrs)	University students and Adults (18yrs+)
Maximum length	Male & female	45 inches (114cm)	46 inches (117cm)	47 inches (120cm)
Minimum weight	Male	16 ounces (440g)	17 ounces (480g)	18 ounces (510g)
	Female	14 ounces (400g)	15 ounces (420g)	16 ounces (440g)
Minimum diameter of sakigawa	Male	1 inch (25mm)	1 ¼ inch (26mm)	1 ¼ inch (26mm)
	Female	¾th inch (24mm)	1 inch (25mm)	1 inch (25mm)
Minimum length of sakigawa	Male and Female	2 inches (50mm)	2 inches (50mm)	2 inches (50mm)

FIK Specifications for Competition use of two Shinai (Nito).			
Specification	Gender	Daito (long shinai)	Shoto (short shinai)
Maximum length	Male & female	45 inches (114cm)	24 inches (62cm)
Weight	Male	16 ounce (440g) minimum	10–11 ounce (280–300g) maximum
	Female	14 ounce (400g) minimum	8–10 ounces (250–280g) maximum
Minimum diameter of sakigawa	Male	1 inch (25mm)	¾th inch (24mm)
	Female	¾th inch (24mm)	¾th inch (24mm)

These lengths are however generally referred to by the old Japanese shaku and sun measurement; 3.7, 3.8, and 3.9 equate respectively to 45 inches (114cm), 46 inches (117cm) and 47 inches (120cm). Although there appears to be no regulation banning longer or shorter shinai for practice, these sizes are used universally in everyday training. In competition it is acceptable to shorten a shinai given that it still reaches the regulated weight.

Although length and weight are regulated, there is still a wide choice of shinai styles. The two main types are dobari and koto. Dobari shinai are shaped with a bulge below the tsuba and tend to feel lighter than the traditional koto shinai, which has a straight blade or jinbu and where the balance is more toward the tip.

Shinai styles

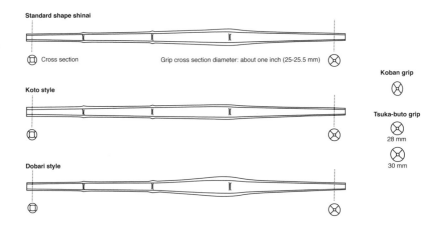

Other options are based around handle size and shape. Round handles are the norm but koban or oval handles are also available. These feel more like using a katana and tend not to accidentally slip round in your hands. The obvious disadvantage is that as the individual *take* are of uneven sizes, it is harder to repair a koban shinai by substituting a single *take*.

There is also a wide variety of grip diameters. Many shinai makers have started to make a variety of "fat handles" to fit bigger hands. Some of these are a little too big for all but the most ham fisted. It is best to choose a grip size that comfortably fits your hand but leaves room for you to maneuver with your tenouchi.

The length of the handle or tsuka is important as this can affect your cutting action. The tsuka should fit in the crook of your right arm so that when you grip it your index finger should be just below the tsuba. Many shinai come complete with leather fittings, but in cases where the bamboo and the fittings are bought separately, many kendoka will purchase a 3.8 tsukagawa for a 3.9 shinai. The tsukagawa tends to stretch in keiko and may need shortening at some stage. In some cases this can be done by turning the front of the tsukagawa back, but in others it is easier to cut and reclose the hilt end.

Depending on source of the bamboo and whether shinai are machine or handmade there is a wide variety of price. The most expensive can be 10 times the cost of the cheapest. Japanese grown madake shinai command a premium price as bamboo grown in colder climates tends to be denser and stronger than that grown in hotter Southeast Asian countries. It is sometimes possible to tell the source of bamboo by the number of ridges on the shinai as cold climate bamboo grows slower.

Unfortunately there is no guarantee that an expensive shinai will last longer than a cheap one.

If, on the other hand, you need a long lasting shinai, you can always purchase a carbon fiber version. These are comparatively expensive but seldom break or go out of shape. The potential disadvantages are that they are less flexible and responsive than bamboo.

Shinai Maintenance

Shinai should be regularly examined for splinters and sanded if they appear. You should also check the inside of the *take* for cracks and splits. If a *take* is damaged it should be replaced. For this reason many people buy shinai in pairs of the same size and configuration so that they can marry the *take*. In my experience though, these "Frankenshinai" seldom last long.

There are a variety of views on oiling and waxing shinai to prolong their life. I believe that it helps to keep the shinai for a few months before use, as this gives it time to adjust to the local humidity. As mentioned, you can buy shinai with or without the leather fittings. There are pros and cons to buying them with or without. If you buy with fittings, a professional shinai maker or bogu shop will use a machine to ensure a good fit for the tsukagawa. Buying the bamboo only, allows you to examine the shinai for uniformity of thickness. If you buy the bamboo and parts separately or take the shinai apart to make repairs, here is what you need to do to tie or retie the parts.

Tying the Sakigawa

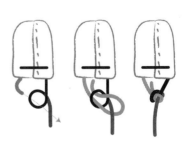

Pull the tsuru through the left hole and loop over the top of the sakigawa passing through the right hole.

Make a loop with the long part of the Tsuru.

Pull the other end through the loop then over and under the descending string

Take back though the loop and pull tight.

Tying the Nakayui

It should be tied one quarter of the total shinai length from the kisaki.

Loop nakayui over taut tsuru by pulling through the slot cut in the end. (In version 2 you can change the nakayui without untying the tsuru by pulling the end of the nakayui through the slot in the other end.)

Wind three times around the *take* and pull back under the last turn.

Take backwards and forwards in a figure of eight (2 or 3 times).

Secure by tucking under the top of the tied nakayui and cut off excess.

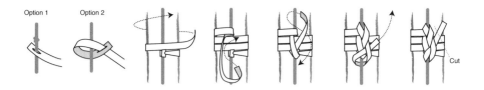

Tying the Tsukagawa (one of several ways depending on fitting)

Make a loop in the tsuru and pull through a second loop pulling tight.

Pass loose end through "v" of leather fitting on tsukagawa.

Take back through loop in tsuru taking over and under straight part of leather fitting and pulling tight.

Take under tsuru, pull up to top of leather "v," compressing it by winding string around and continue to do so, so that it is covered.

Pull end through taught tsuru and tie in a knot, cutting surplus string and pushing the end under the wound string.

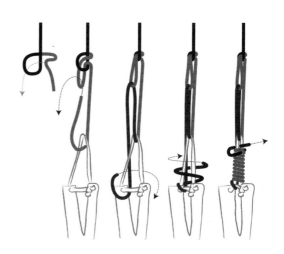

Reigi

"Kendo begins and ends with rei."

The above statement works on two levels; we begin and finish each practice with a bow and kendo is built on the ethos of respect and courtesy.

You will hear the term reigi continually throughout your kendo career, but to clarify terminology, reigi refers to the spirit of respect and courtesy and reiho or reigi saho, its physical expression. Reigi does not just apply to our behavior in the dojo, but should be part of our day to day interaction with others. I, like many other kendo students, was taught that washing the dojo floor and packing and carrying sensei's equipment are an integral part of learning kendo.

In order to understand kendo etiquette, it is necessary to acknowledge two principles: first is the concept of sempai and kohai (senior and junior). Sempai is responsible for the safety and well being of kohai and kohai defers to sempai by sitting in a lower position in the dojo. The relationship is one of mutual respect that must be earned.

Second is the premise that the dojo itself is a sacred place. In the past, a dojo may have been attached to a daimyos' castle or a religious shrine; in some cases they were extensions to the home of the head of the fencing school. In Japan, many of these traditional dojo still exist, although some have been replaced by halls in sports-centers or floors of high rise buildings. In all cases they retain the spirit and the trappings of a traditional dojo. Most have a small kamidana (Shinto shrine) and many have a taiko drum to signal the beginning and end of practice. For western kendoka, it is sometimes difficult to treat an unadorned school or civic hall with the same level of respect, but floors should be swept and ideally washed before each practice session.

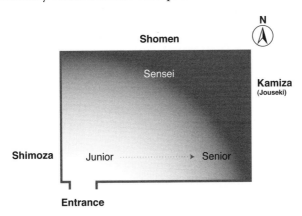

Dojo layout

Dojo layout and the positions where people sit in the dojo can be quite complex. While kendo is practiced around the world in a variety of sports or civic halls, layout is based on traditional Japanese dojo rules where Kamiza faces south and is often located at the furthest point from the door. Members line up in level of seniority on the shimoza side, with the most senior students closest to joseki at the eastern end of the dojo. If there is more than one instructor present, they will also line up in the same pattern on the kamiza side or in some cases with the most senior person in the center and the next highest grade to his right and the next to his left and so on.

Dojo terminology too can be confusing, with some people avoiding the use of the word "kamiza" in the belief that it means god seat. In most cases the meaning is high seat, the same as the translation of joseki. Nevertheless you will often hear the high side of the dojo referred to as shomen or shinzen, both terms refer to "straight ahead."

There are no rules for which grades sit on which side of the dojo. This depends on who teaches and the respective seniority of members and may change from session to session. For example, in my dojo individuals leading the adult practice change with those who taught the earlier children's practice. Sometimes more senior students are placed in joseki. In the Shudokan dojo of Osaka Castle, 8th dan and above only sit in kamiza with 7th dan placed at the far end at a right angle.

Kendo grades

Like many other martial arts and martial sports, kendo uses a system of kyu and dan grades to measure progress. Kyu grades start at 6th kyu and countdown to 1st kyu. In the UK 6th to 2nd kyu are awarded by the students' own dojo. 1st kyu is a national grade and examinations take place under the national federation.

Dan grades start at 1st dan and rise to 8th dan. Formerly kendo used a system of 1st to 10th dan which was then modified so that 9th dan became the highest grade awarded, subsequently the ceiling stopped at 8th dan. While under the current system 9th dan is no longer awarded, there are a number of surviving 9th dan holders, although unfortunately most are reaching an age where keiko is not always possible.

Internationally 1st to 5th dan is usually regulated by national federations or regional federations in Japan. 6th, 7th, and 8th dan are referred to as kodansha grades and awarded by the All Japan Kendo Federation or one of the three zones of FIK (the International Kendo Federation).

The kendo grading system has undergone a number of transformations. Originally there were 5 dan grades followed by the three shogo of Renshi, Kyoshi, and Hanshi. These are now supplementary to the dan-I system and are awarded by recommendation and examination respectively to 6th, 7th, and 8th dan.

Bowing

We bow when we enter and leave the dojo, at the beginning and end of each session, and to each partner at the beginning and end of each keiko. When we enter the dojo or bow to each other we should make a standing bow, keeping our back straight and arms by our side, bending from the waist. We bow to shomen and to our instructors at an angle of 30 degrees and to our opponents at an angle of 15 degrees. For zarei to start and conclude each session, we begin from the seiza position, placing both hands in front on the floor to form a triangle with the thumb and forefinger of each hand. We then place our forehead directly over the center of the triangle, ensuring that we keep a straight back and that we do not raise our bottom. You should breathe in in the upright position and slowly exhale through the mouth as you lower your torso.

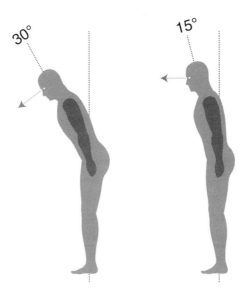

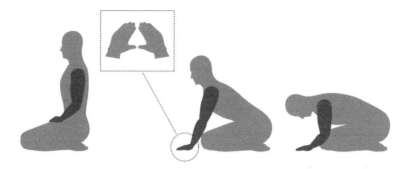

When we bow we should remember that we are not only bowing to our opponent but to those who went before: those who taught us and those who taught them.

Seiza

Seiza may be initially uncomfortable but you get used to it. You should sit with your bottom in the triangle made by your feet. Big toes should be touching or overlapped. Knees should be about two fists distance apart, (together for women) and backs should be straight. Your head should be in a natural position with your chin down.

Mokuso

At the beginning and end of each session we should practice mokuso. We practice this in seiza position with eyes half closed and focussed on the floor about three feet (1 meter) in front of you. The back of one hand should be supported in the palm of the other. Which supports which, is open to debate, so it is basically a matter of choice.

This is a form of meditation to clear our minds before keiko. Mokuso is not full blown zazen, but a way to forget the concerns of the day and ready our minds for training. Some people concentrate on mental images such as the "dark side of the moon" or "looking beyond the mountain." Others concentrate on correct breathing—breathing in quickly through the nose, holding the breath for as long as possible; trying to hold it down with the diaphragm; then breathing out slowly through the mouth.

I personally prefer this approach while thinking:

> Shisei wo tadasu – Correct your posture
> Kokyu wo tadasu – Correct your breathing
> Kokoro wo tadasu – Correct your heart.

Sonkyo

Before each keiko we bow while holding the shinai in our left hand. Our arm should be fully extended downwards holding the shinai below the tsuba at a 45 degree angle. After the bow, we raise the shinai to hip height placing our thumb on the tsuba. This replicates holding the catch mechanism on a katana to stop it being drawn by an opponent.

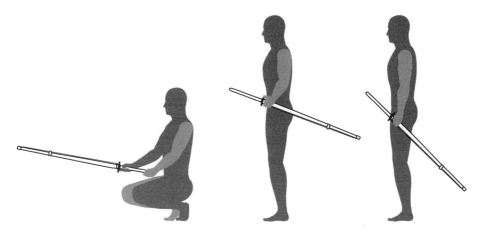

We then take three steps forward and move into sonkyo. Sonkyo is a salutation that only happens in kendo and sumo. When you take the sonkyo position you should do so in a slow and dignified way drawing your shinai at the same time as you assume the position. Knees should be spread widely and back kept straight. Your feet can either be parallel or with the right foot slightly forward so that you are in kamae position when you stand. On standing you should not rush to attack your opponent but try to make "mind contact" to find a suitable attack opportunity.

Other positions

You may from time to time be required to sit on a chair during some kendo events, for example when sitting on a grading panel or waiting to referee. In that case you should maintain an erect posture, keep both feet on the floor and your hands in your lap. Do not slump, cross your legs, or put your elbows on the table.

Commands

The most senior student in each dojo is normally responsible for issuing the commands that govern the reiho at the beginning and end of each session. There are several versions of the command sequence but the most commonly used is:

Opening
- Seiretsu – line up
- Seiza – sit down
- Mokuso – meditation
- Mokuso yame – stop mokuso
- Shomen ni rei – bow to shomen / joseki
- Sensei (sensei gata) ni rei – bow to sensei (plural)
- Men wo tsuke (men tsuke) – put on men and kote

Closing
- Seiretsu
- Seiza
- Men wo torre (men torre) – take off men and kote
- Mokuso
- Mokuso yame
- Sensei ni rei
- Shomen ni rei.

Sometimes confusingly the command "chakuza" is substituted for seiza and seiza for mokuso. In this case the meaning of seiza is different as it refers to sitting quietly.

Reiho dos and don'ts

Do

- Leave your shoes outside the dojo
- Bow as you enter
- Bow to each and every opponent
- Treat every partner, be they senior or junior, with respect
- Give every practice your utmost
- Treat your shinai as you would a real sword
- Listen to sempai or sensei's advice without arguing or justifying your actions
- Pay attention to the condition of your shinai and equipment so that they do not cause injury to others
- Be aware of your position in the dojo line-up
- Be spatially aware, so that you, your partner, or the people practicing near you do not bump into each other or into obstacles in the dojo
- Cross the dojo to thank instructors for their help at the end of the session
- Offer to carry and set out the bogu of teachers or senior visitors
- Be modest and acknowledge successful attacks from your practice partners
- Encourage others.

Don't

- Walk on the dojo floor with shoes on
- Talk in the dojo unless invited to
- Lose your temper if you are hit off-target
- Be rude or arrogant
- Step over other people's shinai
- Use your shinai to strike the floor as a signal to end practice or change partners
- Slouch or lean against the wall when you are waiting to practice
- Cower or use your shinai to avoid being hit; receive the attack gratefully
- Remove your men and kote without being given or asking for permission.

Posture

The effectiveness of your kendo and the speed of your progress will depend on your posture. As this develops, so will your sense of physical well being and physical presence; kendoka are often identifiable by their upright bearing.

You should relax and at the same time try to ensure that you are standing at your full height. Your back should be straight, your chin tucked-in and your feet slightly apart.

From this position you are ready to move into chudan kamae.

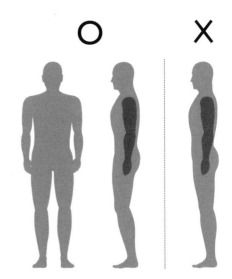

Chudan kamae

Chudan kamae is the most common kamae in modern shinai kendo. This "middle position" when held correctly aligns the point of the shinai with your opponent's nodo or throat, making it impossible for him to strike any of your target points. Chudan kamae also allows you to attack any of the opponent's targets quickly and effectively.

To assume chudan kamae move the right foot forward so that the heel is in line with the big toe of your left foot. Raise the left heel so that is at an angle of about 15 degrees from the floor, placing your weight on the ball of your left foot. As a general rule the width of your stance should be measured by the span of two fists. This, however, varies from person to person.

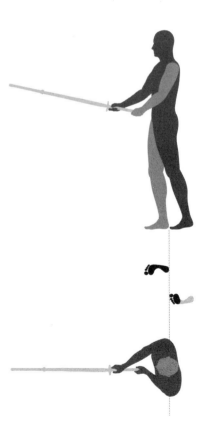

Seventy percent of your weight should be on the ball of your back foot and your left leg should be almost straight. Your right knee should be slightly bent with your right foot lightly touching the floor. Your left hand should be in line with your navel at a 45 degree angle to the floor with your left thumb pointing 12 to 16 inches (30 to 40cm) in front of your right foot. Your right hand should lightly support the shinai and your right thumb should be parallel with the floor.

You should ensure that your shoulders, elbows, and wrists are relaxed and that there is room to raise your arms smoothly without them touching your dou. Your left wrists should be turned in to support the shinai. Your right wrist should be in a natural position with the thumb upwards to facilitate easy movement of the shinai.

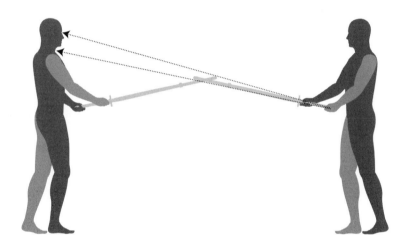

The tip of the shinai can be aimed at any point from your opponent's throat to his right eye.

Holding the shinai

The way that we grip the shinai can make or break our kendo. Grip should be relaxed with the end of  the tsuka inside the left hand and the little, ring, and index fingers supporting the shinai's weight. The forefinger and thumb should apply no pressure, but just be wrapped around the shinai to keep them out of harm's way. The right hand grip should be lighter, again using the little, ring, and index fingers only. The forefinger should be up to a finger's width away from the tsuba. Gripping too tightly and overusing the forefinger means that the shinai will point up too much in chudan kamae and result in striking the bars of the men rather than the top "cushion." Relaxation is the key; someone standing directly in front of you should be able to pull the shinai from your grip without resistance.

I include an old illustration of Mochida sensei's left hand viewed from above and from the front and back of the hand. This picture was included in notes taken by Mr. Sakagami of Nishinomiya Kendo Renmei of a lecture by Matsumoto sensei, hanshi kyudan. The comments that accompanied it described "holding the shinai lightly without squeezing and taking care not to release the little finger. The wrist should be in a straight line without tilting to the right or left."

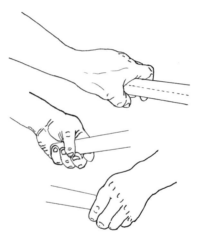

The same lecture notes also highlighted the point that contact with the shinai should be between the finger tips and the heel of the hand with no pressure applied from the base of the fingers.

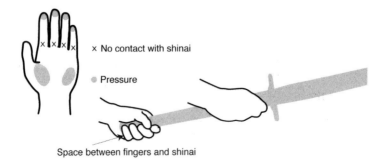

× No contact with shinai

● Pressure

Space between fingers and shinai

Tenouchi

Some kendoka favor a wringing action between the two hands on the point of striking. This tends to put too much stress on the arms and shoulders and spoils both the cut and your posture; instead think about squeezing gently with the three grip fingers of both hands after you strike the target. So if you are striking men, imagine hitting to chin level before you start to squeeze.

Other Kamae

In kendo no kata we practice a number of other kamae in addition to chudan, these are:

Left and right jodan – Where the shinai is held above the head

Left Jodan: Left foot forward   Right Jodan: Right foot forward

Hasso kamae – Similar to jodan but the shinai is held at shoulder height

Waki gamae – The sword is held behind the ride side of the body so as not to be seen by your opponent

Gedan kamae – The sword is pointed down at a 45 degree angle.

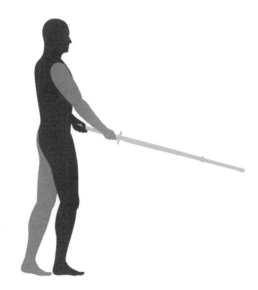

The only one that is commonly used in modern shinai kendo is jodan kamae. This is a highly effective kamae and has been used with great success by a number of top shiai competitors such as Chiba sensei and Toda sensei. In Japanese the word jodan has two meanings, high position and joke. As someone who has no experience of fighting in jodan, an explanation from me is more likely to gravitate towards the second meaning. Gedan may be useful for kendoka if they ever have the rare opportunity to fight against naginata. This happens so rarely that you need not worry too much about it.

On a more serious note it is essential to thoroughly understand chudan no kamae and how to attack correctly from this position before you experiment with other kamae.

Maai

You will often hear the terms Ma and Maai. These are described as Ma being an interval in time and Maai the physical distance between you and your opponent.

Generally kendo distances are classified as toi maai or toma (long distance), issoku ito no maai (one step, one sword distance), and chikai maai (close distance). All are, of course, very important aspects of kendo, but confusing if your question is "which distance should I attack from?" When you

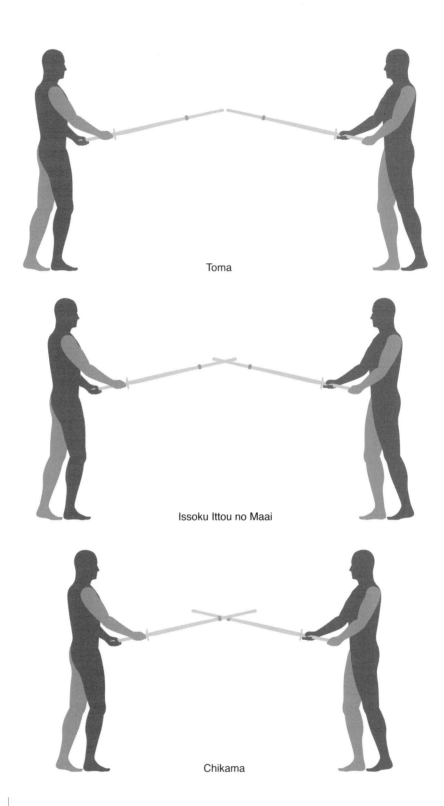

Toma

Issoku Ittou no Maai

Chikama

consider that the farther your distance from your opponent, the less chance of them being able to attack you and the closer your distance the easier it is for you to attack them, then the answer must "as far away as you can be and still make a valid strike in one step."

One theory is that you penetrate the opponent's kensen by six inches (15cm) and if there was no chance to attack, move in another six inches (15cm). Still unable to make an opening, then go back to safe distance and start again. This is a good place to start, but perhaps a little too prescriptive and "one size fits all." Chiba sensei on the other hand talks about "moving as far as you need to into the opponent's distance to break his kamae and to arrive at a point where you can comfortably strike the datotsu-bui with the correct part of the shinai in one step, while retaining good posture.

This is logical and not unique to Chiba sensei. A number of famous kendo teachers, have over the years voiced thoughts along the lines of "everyone has their own distance" or uchima.

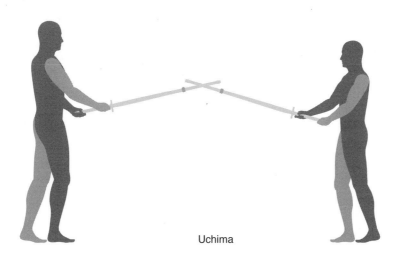

Uchima

So in essence we are talking about your ideal "one step, one cut" distance, which means you have to be in a position to push off from the left foot and in one step cut the correct part of the target. This distance is by no means fixed. We are all different—our own height, weight, leg and arm length, age, and muscle condition will govern the distance we can cover. Remember that your opponent's kote is closer than his men and that dou is farther away. Also remember that the distance for oji-waza is closer, as your opponent is moving forward at the same time; so you need only the smallest of forward movements to make a successful strike.

Like many elements of kendo, the secret of success depends on sharp footwork and you need to practice to ensure that you can vary the distance you cover to suit the opportunity.

Footwork

When we move around in kendo we use suri-ashi or sliding footwork. When we make an attack, in most cases we do so using fumikomi-ashi (stamping footwork).

There are four main types of suri-ashi as follows:

- Ayumi-ashi – sliding footwork where feet cross as in normal walking. Used to cover long distances once maai contact is broken

Ayumi ashi

- Okuri-ashi – sliding footwork where you push off from the left foot and the right foot advances. The left foot is then quickly pulled up so that the toes are in line with the heel of the right foot

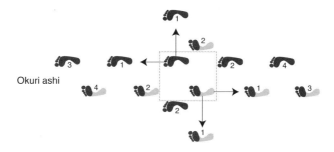

Okuri ashi

- Tsugi-ashi – a less often used footwork where you step forward on the left foot, bringing past the heel of your right foot, but not crossing. This is relatively advanced and is used when making some seme. Because of potential confusion with okuri-ashi it is best not to practice tsugi-ashi until okuri-ashi becomes second nature

Tsugi ashi

- Hiraki-ashi – is used for moving diagonally to the side to affect nuki-waza or oji-kaeshi-waza. With this movement we can move to the left or right of our opponent. To move right we push off from the left foot (again keeping the heel off the ground) and finish at a 45 degree angle to the target with right-foot forward. To move to the left we reverse the process with the left foot forward and the right heel off the ground.

Hiraki ashi

- In all footwork forms the heel of the left foot should remain at a 15 degree angle from and not touch the floor.

Fumikomi-ashi

Fumikomi-ashi is used to make the attack. Once you are in correct distance you push-off from the ball of your left foot and stamp with your right as you strike the target. Your left leg should be almost straight and the motion of your right knee should be forward rather than up. When you stamp, the ball of the right foot should make contact with the floor with the feeling of

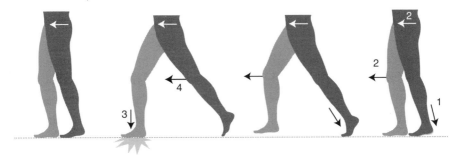

moving forward. It is crucial that you do not lift your right knee too much as this may result in injury from your heel hitting the floor.

Footwork exercises

Footwork or ashi-sabaki can be practiced in individual or group drills and also through suburi. In the case of drills in the dojo, your instructor will call out instructions and you should follow. The idea is to develop your speed and balance so that good footwork becomes second nature.

Foot-care

It goes without saying that finger and toenails should be kept scrupulously short to avoid injury to yourself and your opponent. For your own comfort and to avoid unnecessary breaks in training you should also pay attention to other areas of foot-care.

Hard skin often builds up on kendokas' feet, particular the right foot as a result of fumikomi footwork. If left this skin can sometimes crack and cause ongoing problems. This is more likely to happen in winter when training on cold dojo floors. Although a level of thick skin seems to do no harm and may prevent blisters, hard skin build up should be watched and reduced with a foot file. I find it also helps to use foot moisturisers.

If foot skin is cracked or blistered, it is still possible to train but injuries should be covered. This is not an easy task as most dressings will become detached through friction with the floor. When I trained in Japan, we used a well known brand of tape which when heated with a match or lighter would stay in place for weeks. I am not sure, however, of the hygiene implications of this long term application. A more practical solution would be to wear a tabi or half tabi until the wound heals.

Breathing and Kiai

Breathing technique is important in kendo as is kiai. It is difficult to divorce the two as they are closely connected. As described earlier in the section on mokuso, we breathe in quickly through the nose, hold the breath for as long as possible in the tanden (by tightening the abdominal muscles), and then release the air slowly through our mouth. Kendo utilizes aun-no-kokyu, the yogic or tantric breathing technique that is used in many forms of meditation.

The concept of aun-no-kokyu is that we synchronize breaths with our opponent. Remember that you are vulnerable to attack when you breathe in.

In many cases the out breath can be in the form of kiai or kakegoe. Kiai actually means the meeting of mind /spirit and signifies making mental contact with your opponent. It has, however, come to be accepted as meaning the shout we make before attacking and on striking the target. As an example of how this works, let us take a basic men attack and look at how and when we breathe and use kiai:

- Before you enter attacking distance breathe in quickly and deeply, holding the air in your abdomen
- While still in safe distance make a kakegoe shout expelling half of the retained breath and continuing to hold the remainder
- Step in and strike men, expelling the rest of your breath by shouting "men" as you hit the target. Your kiai should increase in pitch and volume as you go through. This encourages quick movement and good zanshin
- Breathe in again once you are back in safe distance.

Many people worry about developing kiai, thinking consciously about the pitch and the choice of sound used in the preliminary kakegoe. Your kiai should come from the diaphragm and not the throat, so your pitch and tone should be natural and not contrived. In terms of the sounds you use, the best advice is keep it simple; particularly if you are not a Japanese speaker. Single syllables such as ei and ya seldom lead to trouble but more elaborate attempts at kakegoe can be amusing to others. One kendoka was referred to as Santa Claus because of his use of "Ho ho ho!" as a kakegoe.

An excellent way to train your kendo breathing and kiai is through kirikaeshi. The objective should be to strike shomen, four yoko men going forward, five going back, and then follow with one more shomen, all in a single breath. Your kiai should be continuous.

Enzan no metsuke

The sequence of perception to waza in kendo is described as ichi gan, ni soku, san tan, shi riki.

- One – (gan) sight
- Two – (soku) feet

- Three – (tan) abdomen (center / courage)
- Four – (riki) power (technique)

Sight is the first element of any kendo technique and the way that we watch our opponent is crucial to the success of our attack. If we stare at the target we are going to strike, we give our opponent obvious notice of our intention. If we look just at his or her face to try to understand their next action, we may miss the signals he gives when he starts to move hands or feet. If we look just at feet or hands, we can be easily tricked by movement designed to get our attention. If we look at the point of the shinai, there is even more chance that we may be fooled by a feint. We therefore use enzan no metsuke (the way of looking at a far mountain).

Yuko-datotsu

Before moving on to waza, it is worth considering what makes a valid strike or yuko-datotsu in kendo. There are five elements that must be present in the strike. These are:

- Correct posture should be shown
  - The body should be in an upright position with the chin tucked in and shoulders relaxed

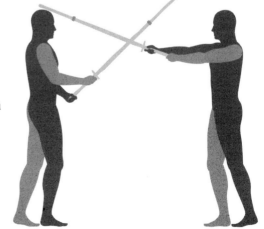

- The correct target should be hit
  - Men – Top of the head

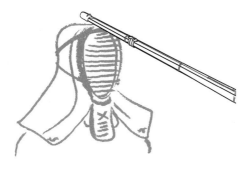

  - Yoko- men – Top left or right hand side of the men

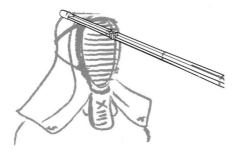

  - Tsuki – The kisaki should strike tsukidate (tsuki pad) of the men

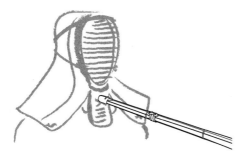

  - Migi-kote – The padded area on the right wrist

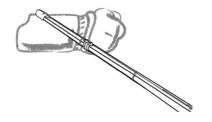

- Hidari-kote - The padded area on the left wrist, only valid if the kote is above shoulder height

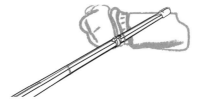

- Dou – The right hand side or front of the dou-plate

- Gyaku-dou - The left hand side of the dou-plate (needs to be stronger and clearer than migi-dou)

- The correct part of the shinai should be used
  - The datotsu-bu or area above the nakayui must strike the target. Also hasuji or angle of the blade should be correct with the *take* furthest from the string of the shinai striking the target

- Intention must be clear
  - You must demonstrate intention. If your opponent's kote comes up and you hit it as you go to strike men, it is not a valid-yuko datotsu, no matter how strong the hit
- Zanshin must be present
  - Once the attack is completed you should go past your opponent and turn, and then stop in safe distance with good kamae. If this is not possible, keep in front of your partner, maintaining strong chudan. You need to remain in control.

CHAPTER 2

Waza

There is a vast kendo repertoire of techniques, but all are based on just FOUR distinct strikes; men, kote, dou, and tsuki. What gives us this variety are the multiple permutations of opportunity and timing allowing the same waza to be used for offense or defense; singly or in combination.

Rather than catalog every possible variation, I intend to deal with each basic strike in detail and then look at the opportunities to deploy it. Kendo techniques are classified as shikake-waza, attacking techniques or oji-waza, defensive techniques. In kendo there is little difference between attack and defense, as your attitude should always be that of pressurizing your opponent and moving forward. Despite the terminology, defensive techniques are best applied by forcing your opponent to attack and then taking away the opportunity and striking him first.

Mitsu No Sen

You will frequently hear the terms sen, sen-no-sen, and go-no-sen. These apply to the timing of attack as follows:

- Sen – attacking before your opponent, for example tobikomi-men
- Sen-no-sen – making your attack as your opponent starts his technique, for example debana men
- Go-no-sen – oji-waza, knocking down, avoiding, or parrying your opponent's technique after he begins his attack and then responding with your own waza.

Shikake Waza

Sutemi

At this point it is worth highlighting one more principle: that of sutemi. In kendo sutemi means that once you commit to making an attack, you do so 100 percent. When you launch yourself into a shikake attack, there should be no thought of stopping or going back.

The term sutemi is commonly understood to mean sacrifice. Literally it means "throw away the seeds" and is taken from a Japanese poem describing seeds in a fast flowing river and their choice of sinking or throwing away the kernels so that the empty husks continue to flow with the current.

Men-uchi

The following description is based on the instructions of the late Matsumoto sensei Hanshi 9th dan–Starting in chudan kamae with the weight distribution 70:30 between left and right feet, the left heel, which is now raised, should be slightly lowered. This will redistribute the weight 50:50 to the back and front of the left sole. The toes of the left foot which have so far pointed slightly to the left should point straight ahead. Now with the motion of stepping out from the left ankle, you should push your right foot forward. Now the tension behind the left knee moves to a point of about 2¼ inches (6cm) above the back of the left knee and tension is applied to a slightly lesser degree to the same point above the right knee, the left hip can then be pushed forward.

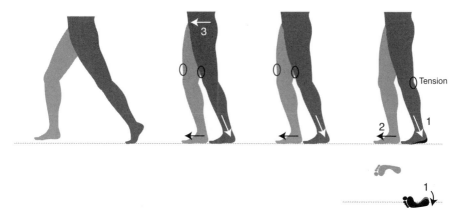

Step within easy reach of your opponent, without changing the position of your hands. The left hand is then raised with the right hand following in

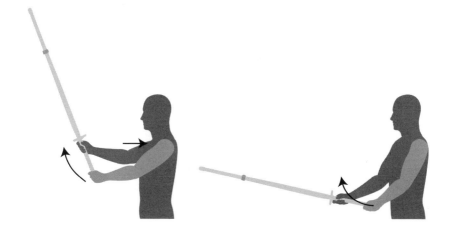

a natural movement in line with the path of the shinai. This action will cause your right shoulder to draw back. At this point the right hand is acting as support to the left and it is wrong to apply force with the right hand in order to raise the shinai. It is important that you raise the right hand with the feeling of squeezing in, which will protect your kote against counterattack as you raise your hand.

You should strike at the same time as you draw the left foot towards the right foot. At this point, the right hand, which so far has not been used to apply force is given the work of hitting together with the left hand, making use of the right elbow to indicate direction. Make maximum use of the power and flexibility of your wrists and use the integral power of your waist, back, shoulders, and arms. When you make the strike the distribution of weight between your left and right legs will change to 40:60.

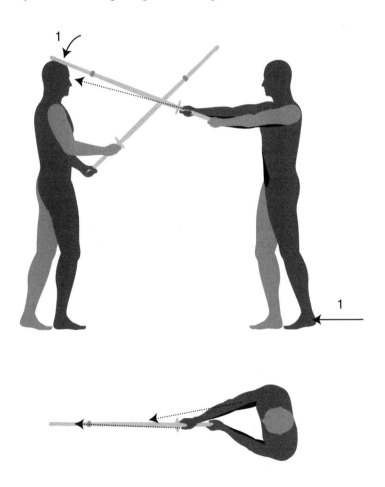

When you strike men, the thumb of the right hand is directed to the front as if to poke into your opponent's eyes.

Zanshin

After striking men it is imperative that you continue to display strong spirit and maintain chudan kamae so that you can defend yourself against possible counterattack. For men this is normally done by taking three or four steps past your opponent keeping the point of the shinai forward and then turning and stepping forward into chudan kamae.

Key points:

- Push yourself forward from your left foot so that you are in correct striking distance
- Do not lift your arms until you start to bring your left foot up
- Your left hand only should power the upswing
- Use your wrists to complete the strike.

Kote-uchi

The previous template for men attack is effectively the basis of all shikake waza. The movement for kote is similar. The key differences are that you do not need to raise the shinai as high as for men and because kote is closer you can attack from greater distance, or take a smaller step to reach the target.

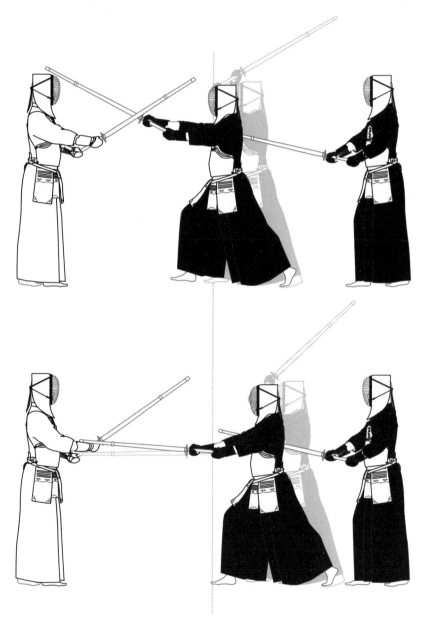

It is critical that the tip of the shinai move in a forward path rather than being pulled backwards. I have heard the movement for kote described as being "like a chameleon's tongue coming out to catch a fly."

Driving with the left hand and keeping your right hand relaxed, you lift your left hand so that it is just above the bars of your own men then you strike your opponent's kote aiming for the point just below the kote, so that the intention is to cut through the thickness of his wrist and no more.

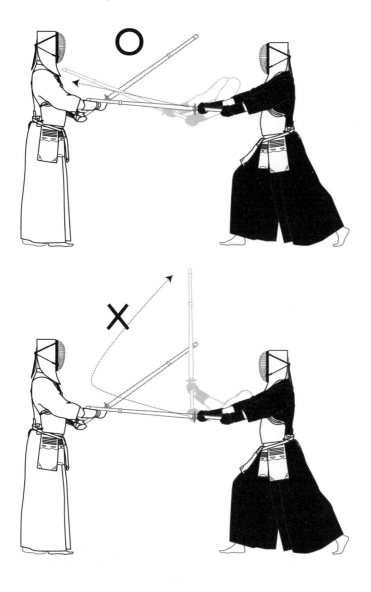

The tenouchi action is as for men, one of gently squeezing the shinai at the point where the cut finishes. Kote in particular needs to be sharp, making a snapping sound as it strikes, so tenouchi is very important.

Because kote requires a smaller cutting action than men you do not need to move your feet as early as for a larger strike.

You also need to adjust your position so that your body is centered on your opponent's kote rather than remaining face-to face. As you move forward you should move your right foot diagonally so that it is in line with his right foot. If you do not do this you will need to strike with your shinai extending diagonally from your center to the target or you will have to move your hands out of line with your own center. Neither of these is correct and the strike would not be judged as a valid yuko-datotsu.

Opponent

Zanshin for kote depends on the velocity of your opponent's and your own forward movement. If you can stop easily, you should do so with the tip of your shinai pointing at his throat. If you can't, you should move into tsubazeriai so that you are immune from a return attack.

Dou Uchi

Dou is practiced in drills as a shikake technique but tobikomi dou is seldom used in keiko or shiai. If your opponent is in chudan kamae then his arms are by his side, making dou difficult to hit. You therefore need to strike dou when his arms are raised. This means that dou is attempted most often as an oji waza, either as nuki dou or kaeshi dou. Both of these require you to move diagonally in front of your opponent although your position at the time of striking is different.

We are often taught to make the dou strike from above men height, striking at a 45 degree angle to the right side of our opponent's dou. Many kendoka find this difficult and the result is that the shinai slips either down towards the floor or trails across the front of the dou. I believe that instead of aiming for this 45 degree angle, we should turn our wrists at the moment of striking so that the bottom *take* makes full contact with the target. It helps to make a conscious effort to push the right hand forward at the point of impact.

Because we are effectively cutting diagonally across our opponent's body, we need to change our grip on the shinai as we go through. There are two ways to do this; either slide the left hand up the tsuka, so that it joins the right hand, or release the left hand completely so that the shinai does not impede your movement. You should continue to watch your opponent as you move through to safe distance.

Slide   Open

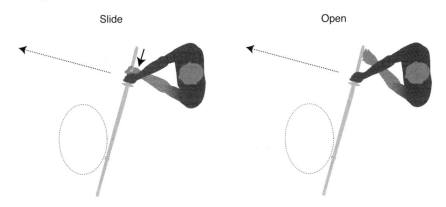

Whereas kote is closer than men, dou is farther, so you need to take either a bigger step in to reach the target, or launch your attack from a closer position.

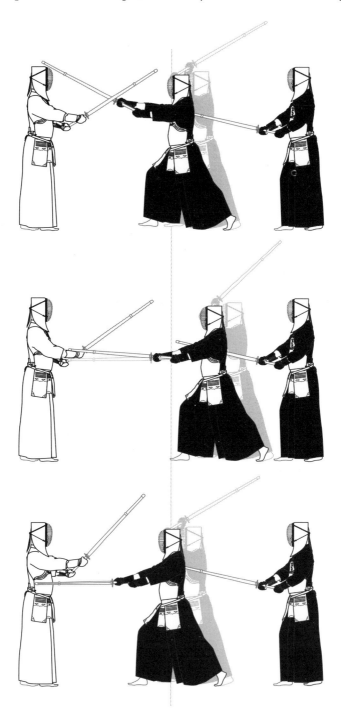

Gyaku-dou

Gyaku-dou is an effective technique that almost always surprises the receiver. The technique is executed to left side of the dou and is usually performed as a hiki-waza, with the attacker stepping back on the left foot as the shinai strikes. The cutting motion is also that of hiki-giri with the left hand being pushed forward before the strike and then being pulled in towards your own abdomen. The zanshin for this technique is the assumption of chudan kamae as you step into safe distance.

To be effective gyaku-dou requires a stronger strike than migi dou and extra attention to ensure that hasuji (angle of the blade) is correct as, traditionally, the shorter sword of the daisho worn by samurai would be worn in their belt and have to be cut through as part of a successful left dou attack.

Tsuki

Tsuki is one of the four valid targets, but is ignored by many kendo authors and instructors. This is because it is difficult to do well and it can be potentially dangerous. It should not be practiced until you are confident that you can control your movement and balance. However, once you are able to do it safely you should practice both morotetsuki (two handed) and katatetsuki (one handed).

Morotetsuki

It is important that you do not just attack tsuki by pushing your hands forward. Instead you should step forward from your left foot and start to push both hands forward as your right foot touches down. Your left hand should provide the power for the thrust and you should turn both hands in, concentrating on hitting the cross in the center of your opponent's tsuki pad as you make hikitsuke by bringing up your left foot so that the toes line up with the heel of your right foot. The strike should be sharp and you should pull back as soon as you hit the target and not continue to apply forward pressure.

Katatetsuki

The body movement for this one-handed tsuki is similar, but you gain more reach by pushing forward with your left hand only. The left hand should twist in a corkscrew motion so that thumb is pointed down on impact. As you launch the thrust you should pull your right hand onto your hip to stabilize your body. Again the attack should be a sharp "on-off." It is important that the end of the tsuka sits inside your hand and is supported by the heel of your hand so that your hand does not slip forward on impact.

Tsuki is a proactive attack. While a training partner may accidentally run into your kamae, it is unforgiveable to attempt mukaetsuki against an opponent who is moving forward.

Timing and Opportunity for Shikake Waza

Having looked at the four main attacking techniques, the challenge is to understand when to use them. Shikake waza and the opportunity at which they are used can be classified as follows:

- Tobikomi waza – attacking at your own timing when you see a clear target
- Hikibana waza – forcing your opponent to retreat and hitting when he is off-guard
- Debana waza – attacking at the point when your opponent is beginning to launch his attack
- Harai waza – creating an opening by sweeping your opponent's shinai to the side
- Osae waza - creating an opening by pushing your opponent's shinai to the side or down
- Uchiotoshi waza – creating an opening by knocking your opponent's shinai down
- Makiotoshi / makiage waza – disarming your opponent by wrapping your shinai around his and throwing it down or up
- Renzoku waza – launching continuous successive attacks to break your opponents composure
- Hiki waza – Attacks moving backwards from tsubazeriai.

Tobikomi Waza

Basic attacks using techniques already described to a clear target at our own timing. These waza are used in drills and in jigeiko when we see an obvious opportunity.

Hikibana Waza

We will look at seme a little later, but hikibana opportunities present themselves as a result of us stepping into our opponent's distance and causing his kamae or concentration to break and forcing him to step backwards.

Debana Waza

Debana men

Debana men is the "holy grail" of kendo. It is the most desirable waza to display in high dan grading examinations and enbu.

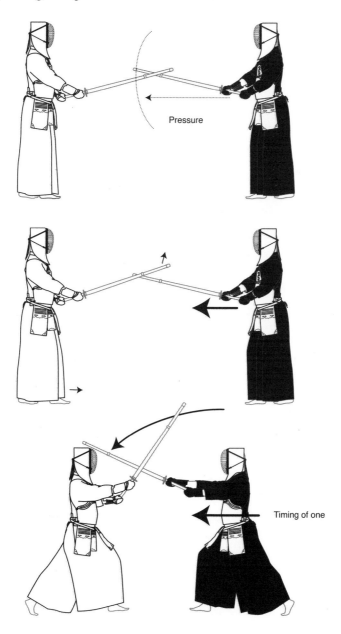

In my view, the reason why it is such a special technique is that it requires the ability to attack instantly, without conscious thought in the spirit of "mushin."

To effectively achieve debana men, your preparation needs to be perfect. You must be in your own uchima, have a feeling of pressure between your kisaki and your opponent's, have your left heel off the ground and a 70:30 distribution of weight between your left and right foot. As soon as your opponent starts his attack, you should push forward from your left foot and strike in the "timing of one." Effectively, you are making the down stroke while your opponent is starting his upward raise. Normally the attacker should take the initiative, making seme into the distance, and then keep in tame (the feeling of applying continued pressure from your center) until your opponent's concentration wavers.

This is clearly a technique that calls for repeated practice. One simple drill for this is, working with a partner, move into issoku ito maai. Both hold the strongest chudan that you can and build up a feeling of pressure. Ensure that your feet are in correct kendo position and that the left heel is up and the weight balance is as described. Motodachi should wait until the feeling of pressure between you is palpable and then quickly lean slightly forward while lifting the shinai to the right and moving the right foot forward by just a few inches. As soon as he does this kakarite should attack men instantly, pushing off from the left foot.

Degote

From isoku ito ma, raise the point of your shinai to the right, in the direction of your opponent's left eye. This should be only a slight movement. You need do no more than squeeze gently with the little finger of your right hand to make the point move. As you do this, it is likely, (although not guaranteed), that your opponent will see the chance to hit your men and start to lift his shinai. As soon as he does this, push off from your left foot and hit kote. The footwork and weight distribution should be the same as for debana men, but because kote is closer, you should not have to travel as far forward. Do not wait until his hand is in the air, you should strike at the beginning of his move so that although you now see the target, it should still be parallel with the ground.

Degote is a small technique, but do not make the mistake of just using your left hand as a pivot and pushing with your right. You should try to lift your left hand and throw it forward, taking your right hand with it. Do not

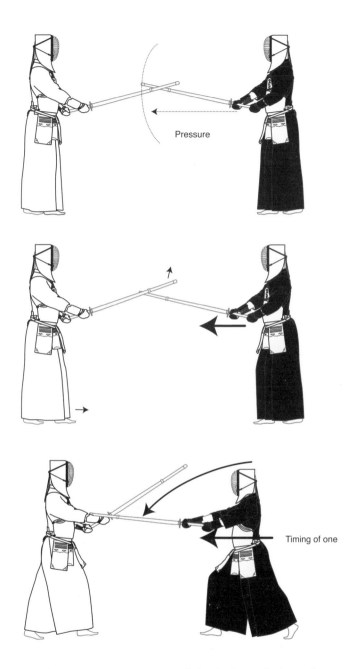

Pressure

Timing of one

have the feeling of chopping down. Instead think about flicking the point out and forward like a chameleon's tongue catching a fly. Also your body should be square on to your opponent's kote. It helps to move your right foot across the center line as you attack so that you finish with the toes of your right foot in line with the toes of your opponent's right foot.

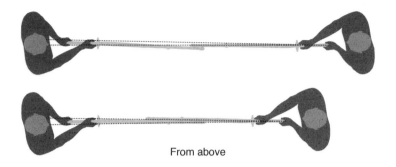

From above

Finally your zanshin should be correct, either pointing your shinai to the opponent's center, or if one or both of you is moving forward quickly, stop in tsubazeriai. Do not spoil the technique by twisting or ducking. Keep your posture.

Harai Waza

With harai waza you step into distance and create an opening by sweeping or knocking your opponent's shinai to the side. This can be done for both kote and men. The harai technique should be sharp and be created by a snapping motion using the wrists of both hands to deflect the shinai. The feeling should be that of creating a sharp wringing action in the direction in which you are hitting your opponent's shinai. Do not use the power of your shoulders to sweep the shinai, otherwise you risk breaking your own kamae and giving your opponent the chance to attack.

It is essential that the strike to men or kote follows immediately after you deflect the shinai and the sweep and strike are done in one step.

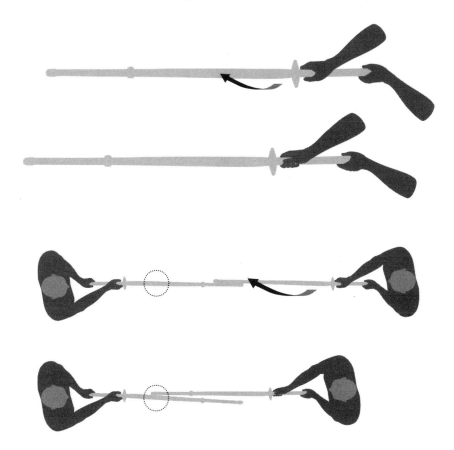

Harai men can be applied to either omote or ura and the shinai can be deflected to the side or up or down diagonally depending on your opponent's height and the position of his kamae. Harai techniques work best against opponents who grip the shinai tightly.

Harai gote

A good opportunity to attack harai-gote is when your partner is retreating, either because you are making a strong forward seme, or because you have just failed in another forward attack. Under the circumstances, he is often on his back foot and does not have complete control of the shinai. In this situation, harai-gote is easier to apply than men. As you are already in close distance, you are able to strike the shinai at the tsuba end of the blade, which has maximum effect in moving the point from center. Also harai to the ura (kote side) of the shinai is more forceful as you are knocking the shinai out of the grip of your opponent's right hand (you are hitting in the direction of his open fingers from the back of his hand). With a harai strike to omote for men, you are pushing the shinai further into his right hand.

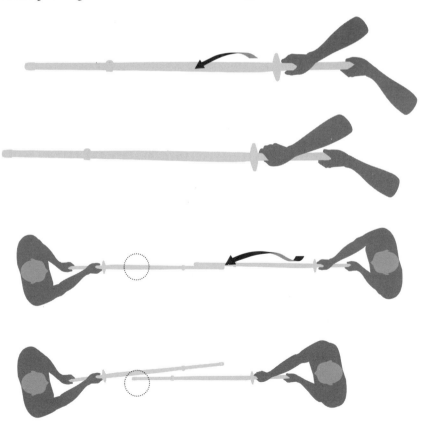

Osae Waza

Osae waza are used to push the opponent's shinai out of position by applying firm pressure from the tip of your shinai. In this way the shinai can be pushed down or to the side allowing you to make a rapid attack to men or kote when it leaves the center line. Osae can be used in reverse by pushing against your opponent's kamae and forcing him to push back. As he does so, drop the point of your shinai and hit the target as he continues to push past the center point. This is a particularly good way of forcing your partner to open his kote to attack.

Uchiotoshi

Uchiotoshi is the act of hitting your opponent's shinai from above to knock it down.

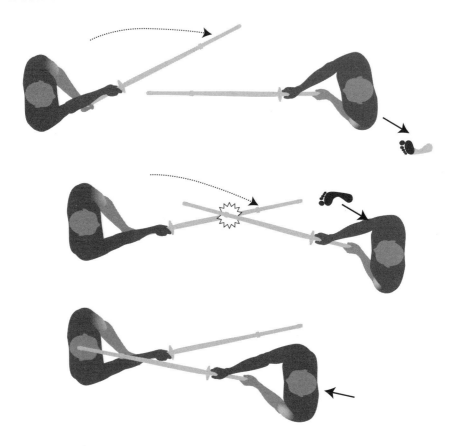

    The mechanics of the technique are similar to harai waza. Uchiotoshi is also used as an oji technique to respond to a dou attack.

Makiotoshi and Makiage

This is the process of wrapping the jinbu of your shinai around that of your opponent and then throwing his shinai down or upwards. This technique is seldom used, but when it is and done well, it can be particularly spectacular. I had the pleasure of watching a shiai in which Hotta sensei of Hyogo Police flicked his opponent's shinai out of his hands to a height where it hit the roof beams of the old Osaka Central Gymnasium.

Maki-age from Omote   Maki-otoshi from Omote

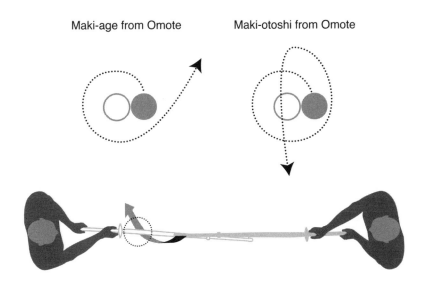

Renzoku Waza

Renzoku waza are continuous attacks sometimes called after the number of techniques in the sequence such as nidan or sandan waza. Many people believe that in sequences such as kote men, the first kote attack is not meant to succeed, but rather is intended to set up your opponent for the following men-strike. I, perhaps simplistically, feel that you should try to hit kote and if you miss, then you should continue on to strike men. If your opponent is going backwards and his posture is breaking under the pressure of your attack, but you are unable to make a clear point then you continue to push forward striking continually until you succeed. Kote, men, dou, tsuki—all can be put together in any combination, but to work they require perfect ki-ken-tai-itchi and one step per cut.

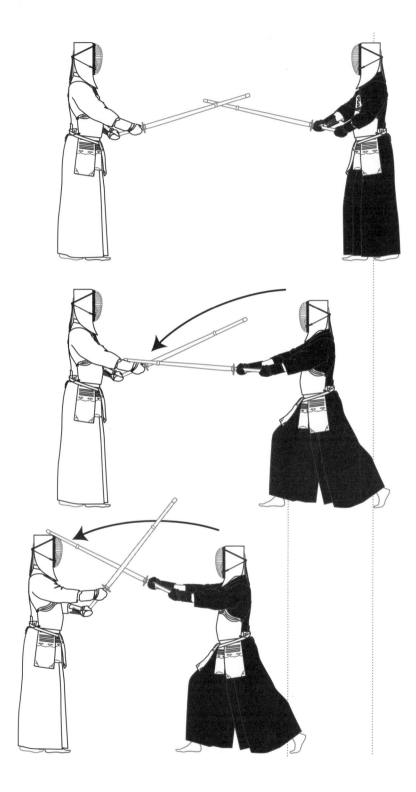

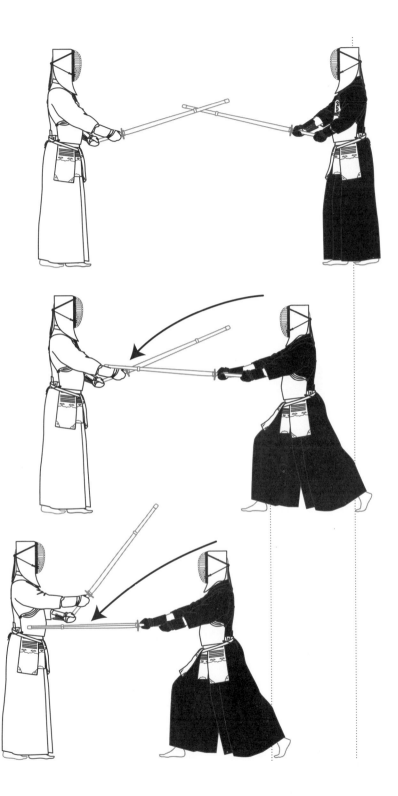

Hiki Waza

Hiki waza fall into the category of shikake waza but are almost a class of technique on their own. Hiki waza are techniques made going backward from tsubazeriai. Men dou and kote can be done in this way. Only tsuki is not a viable hiki technique.

To get to tsubazeriai in the first place we normally push into close distance with our opponent using taiatari, so it is probably worth briefly describing how this should be done.

If, after making a forward attack, your opponent is still directly in front of you pull your shinai towards your body and push forward using your hips. The secret to successful taiatari is not to compromise your posture. After hitting, keep your arms and shoulders relaxed, drop your hands into correct tsubazeriai, keep your balance between your feet and slightly drop your hips forward. This should be enough either to move your opponent, or at least to put you in safe, close distance, ready to make your next move.

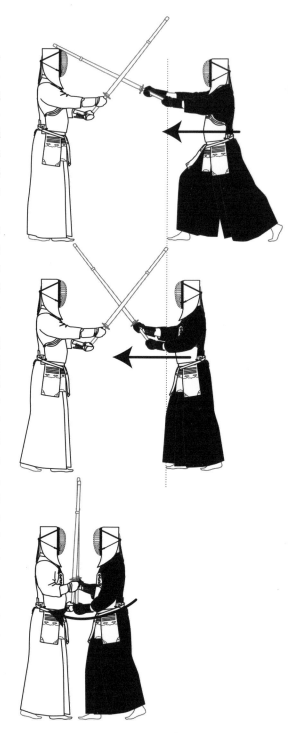

Tsubazeriai

In tsubazeriai the omote side of the jinbu of the shinai should be crossed at the point above the tsuba. The shinai should not directly touch your opponent. Any variation to the above is classed as a tsubazeriai infringement and would earn a hansoku in shiai.

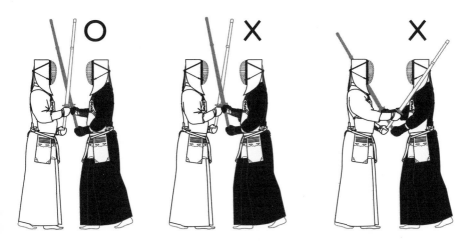

Hiki men

From tsubazeriai push your partner's hands upwards. As he responds by pushing down he exposes his men. Lean back slightly and step back with your left foot, making sure that you create sufficient distance to strike the men with the datotsu bu of your shinai. As you strike men you should pull your right foot back, making fumikomi. Zanshin should take the form of you continuing to move back to safe distance, keeping your shinai in chudan position.

Hiki gote

This time push your opponent's hands to your left so that he pushes back to your right, opening his kote for attack. Moving in the same way as for hiki men, step back and strike kote. Remember that as his kote moves forward into kamae it is closer than men, so you will need to create sufficient distance.

Hiki men

Hiki gote

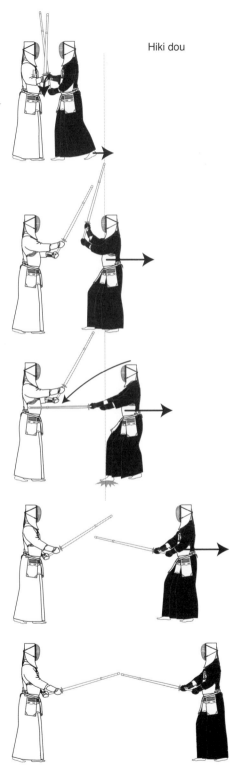

Hiki dou

Hiki dou

Again the process is the same. This time push his hands down and hit dou as he forces them up against your pressure.

Seme Tame and the Four Sicknesses

The waza described above have been developed to break through another's defences. All of them incorporate ways to unsettle an opponent and rely on exploiting the four kendo sicknesses (shi kai) of surprise, fear, doubt, and hesitation.

In addition to the ways described to physically break through your opponent's defences you will constantly hear reference to the terms "seme" and "tame" which are used to break your opponent's equilibrium.

Seme is the root of semeru which literally means to attack, but in kendo it is the accepted term for breaking through your opponent's defense and taking the center. The importance of seme cannot be underestimated. It is said that you win with seme and the strike that follows is just confirmation. I have seen examples of this where high ranking kenshi have acknowledged defeat on the basis of their opponent breaking through their kamae.

There are two major opportunities to attack. One when your opponent makes his own attack. Two when he succumbs to the pressure of your forward movement. In each case you need to be confident and full of spirit, while keeping your mind clear and level. In the first instance you stop and hold your pressure "tame," just moving the point of your shinai enough to invite an attack and then hit as he is about to start his technique. This is debana waza. If his attack is more advanced then you use oji waza.

The second option is easier to understand. You simply step in and take center (you can do this if he steps back or forward). As his kamae breaks you strike (shikake waza). This is the most obvious example of seme. You do not need to push his shinai with your own, but simply step in strongly with good kamae and dominate with the strength of your ki or spirit (kizeme).

Sansappo or Sansatsuho -
The Three Ways of Making an Opening:

- *Ki wo korosu* - Kill the spirit / mind
- *Ken wo korosu* - Kill the sword
- *Waza wo korosu* - Kill the technique

You will also hear reference to the concept of sansappo (Three ways of making an opening).

The first two relate to shikake waza. The first uses seme, the second moves the opponent's shinai, and the third relates to oji waza which we will deal with next.

- *Ki wo korosu* - Take a deep step into your opponent's distance with full spirit. The movement has to be deep and aggressive. Merely pushing in past the point of his shinai is not enough. The movement must be sufficiently strong to break his composure and force him to lose the center. As soon as he does this, strike *men*.

- *Ken wo korosu* - In essence this means to knock the shinai out of the center, so *harai, osae, uchiotoshi,* or *makiotoshi* can all justifiably claim to fit this purpose.

- *Waza wo korosu* - This means to break the attack against you and counter, so debana, oji, kaeshi, nuki, suriage, etc. all fall into this category. The key point here is not to wait, but to aggressively force or invite your opponent to attack and take away and return his waza.

CHAPTER 3

Oji Waza

Oji waza is the term for counter techniques in kendo. We do not, however, passively wait to respond to our opponent's reaction; our attitude should be that of aggressive attack and in most cases we actively force our opponent to make the first move so that we can deploy these techniques. The techniques you use should not only depend on your own preference, but should be selected with a view to the height, strength, and attacking style of your opponent.

Oji waza include the following:

- Nuki waza – Avoiding techniques, where you move your body out of the opponent's line of trajectory and respond with your own strike

- Suriage waza (sliding up techniques) –Where you deflect your opponent's shinai by sliding your shinai along their descending blade and strike at your target on your way down

- Kaeshi waza (more correctly ojikaeshi waza) – Here you block on one side of their shinai and instantly return the attack to a target on the other side

- Uchiotoshi waza – Similar to a shikake waza, but this time you knock the opponent's shinai down as he attacks and respond with your own attack.

Men Nuki Men

The first technique in Kendo no kata. When practiced as a shinai kendo drill, motodachi attempts a big shomen attack. Kakarite steps diagonally to the right (motodachi's left side), and then steps forward to execute men uchi. Theoretically this technique can also be done stepping to the left or as in the kata backward and forwards to strike. In the former it is difficult to maneuver your shinai on motodachi's ura side, with the latter it is unlikely you can find sufficient distance to avoid his men strike. It is crucial that after you hit men you move forward with strong spirit.

Kote Nuki Men

For me, this is a more obvious, more practical nuki technique. Motodachi attacks kote, you simply lift your kote avoiding his downward strike and return the strike to men. This can be done while directly in front of your opponent, going forward as for a shikake technique.

Kote Nuki Kote

This works when motodachi moves to the ura side of your shinai to hit your kote. As he strikes you lift your right hand above his shinai While stepping to the left in an "hiraki ashi" step, striking immediately once you are in line with his kote.

Men nuki dou

Motodachi attacks your men; as the shinai reaches men height, push forward from the back foot, moving diagonally across your opponent's path. As you do so move your hands forward, with the left hand providing the power to strike dou. While your body moves diagonally, your hands should move in a forward direction turning to hit the right side of your opponent's dou. As you move forward to turn into zanshin you should either move your left hand up to join your right or release with your left hand.

Men Suriage Men

As motodachi attacks men, you slide your shinai upwards against his blade deflecting the strike and hitting his men on the down stroke. The sliding motion upwards is often described as your shinai making a "D" shape, but I find

that if you push up with the shinogi (shoulder of the shinai), the taper of your shinai is sufficient to make the opening. The technique can be performed to omote or ura stepping diagonally to the left or right. It can also be done to the omote side in a straight line. In this case, you sweep up as you push off from your left foot and slide up the shinai as your right foot touches the floor and strike as you bring your left foot up.

Suriage men will only work if you keep the point of your shinai forward for both the slide up and the strike. Do not pull your point back. It is also critical that your opponent's men attack is correct in both direction and timing, otherwise your suriage will not be effective.

Tsuki Suriage Men

Suriage men is also an effective defence against tsuki. In fact it is easier to practice as a drill, as motodachi has no opportunity to move his shinai away from a central position.

Kote Suriage Men

As motodachi attacks your kote, move your left foot to the left while turning the shinai so that your thumb is parallel with the floor. Continue to lift the point of the shinai pushing up with your left hand and strike as soon as the kisaki is above your opponent's head. As you strike make a forward fumiko-mi stamp with your right foot.

Kote Suriage Kote

This technique is similar to kote suriage men, except that your strike in response to kote is delivered to the opponent's right kote. Because this target is closer than men, you need to create more distance as you step to the side or diagonally with your left foot and make the forward step with your right foot smaller than in the case of men. It may not be possible to make fumikomi. If so, rely on suriashi footwork. Your kote strike needs to be instantaneous; otherwise your partner will recover his kamae and protect his kote.

Men Kaeshi Dou

Men kaeshi dou is initially difficult to master, but is a highly effective technique, favored by many kendo high grades. The key component to success is that you block and return the attack in the "timing of one."

As motodachi strikes men, kakarite blocks by raising his shinai, pushing the point forward, as he blocks with the omote side. As he blocks, he pushes forward from the left foot, moving the right foot to the diagonal right. Then driving from the left hand, he changes the angle of the right hand so that the thumb rotates downwards towards the floor and his shinai moves from omote to ura and strikes the right side of motodachi's dou. At the point of striking, kakarite should be directly in front of motodachi, bringing up the left foot on completion of the strike and pushing strongly forward with the left hip. After hitting, kakarite moves diagonally in front of motodachi to the right (motodachi's left). This can be done either in suri ashi footwork or the step after the strike can be made in ayumi / aruki ashi, crossing the left foot in front of the right as in the 7th movement of kendo no kata.

The shinai must be pulled through as previously described, either by sliding the left hand forward on the tsuka to meet the right, or by releasing the left hand completely. Remember to keep eye contact.

Men Kaeshi Men

Using the kaeshi movement already described (and again ensuring that you keep the kisaki pointing forward), you can perform kaeshi men moving to either the left or right side. You block the attack on the shinai's shinogi and return to attack yoko men on the other side. In the case of hidari men, you block on omote side when you are positioned directly in front of your opponent and return the strike as you move to the left. Using hiraki ashi footwork you step to the left with your left foot, closing with your right as you strike. This process is reversed for kaeshi migi men. Kaeshi men (particularly to right men) may not work with a taller opponent as his kamae may impede the strike.

Kote Kaeshi Kote

In my view the most difficult of the kaeshi waza because of the close distance inherent on attacking kote. This is effectively a hiki waza, where you need to step back to create the room to make a valid kote strike.

As your opponent strikes kote you raise your shinai to block on the right shinogi, making a big diagonal step back on your left foot, you reverse the position of your shinai from omote to line up with his kote in ura, striking as you pull your right foot into line with your left. For zanshin you should take one more step back with your shinai in chudan kamae.

Dou Uchiotoshi Men

We looked at uchiotoshi as a shikake waza, but this technique can be used equally effectively as a counter. In this instance motodachi attacks kakarite's dou. Kakarite steps back diagonally on the left foot bringing up the right foot as he hits motodachi's shinai down. He then pushes forward from the left foot to strike men as he steps forward with the right and goes forward into zanshin.

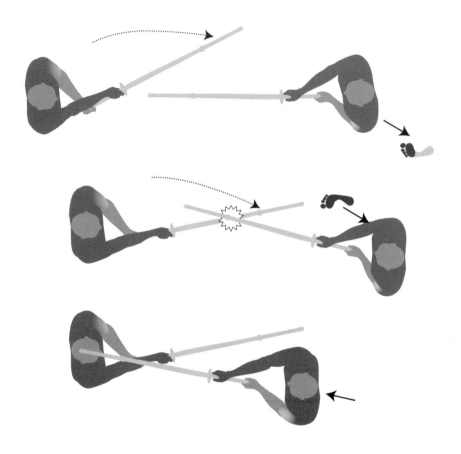

Tsuki Nayashi Tsuki

As per kata number three, we react to motodachi's tsuki by pushing our hands forward to deflect the thrust as we step back (left, right), as his shinai breaks the center we quickly step in and return the tsuki.

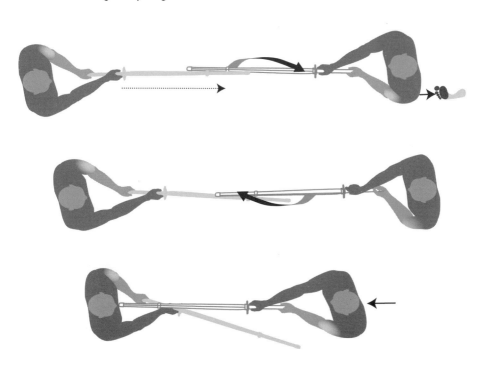

Footwork for Oji Waza

It is worth bearing in mind that in the lead up to most oji waza, your opponent is moving forward. You therefore do not need to take big forward steps or use the same amount of forward momentum as if you were initiating shikake waza. As a rule of thumb 50 percent of the movement used for shikake waza will result in a successful oji strike.

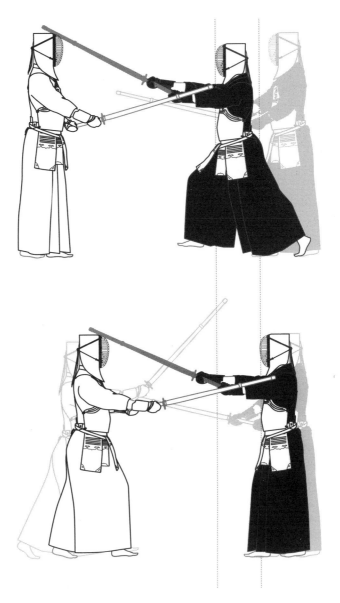

CHAPTER 4

Kendo Training Methods

Kihon Geiko

Many kendoka mistakenly assume that the continued practice of basic techniques is only for beginners. This is not the case. Because of the complexity of seme, timing, and opportunity required to make a successful strike in jigeiko, it is easy to let the quality of your technique and posture deteriorate if your training only concentrates on winning points.

Basic technique and movement should be practiced throughout your kendo career up to and including the senior dan ranks. This is particularly true for times when you are "facing a wall." In this case it always pays to go back to basics.

Motodachi Geiko and Mawari Geiko

Kendo training exercises are often collectively referred to as kihon geiko or basic practice. A list of the most common forms of kihon geiko follows. These exercises can be practiced in a number of ways. The most common are as motodachi geiko, where an instructor or senior acts as receiver or as mawari geiko, where students of similar level take turns at receiving and attacking as they move around in two opposing lines changing partners on an instructor's command. The exercises described can be practiced singly and repeated with each change of partner or arranged in a sequence such as kirikaeshi, jigeiko, and uchikomi geiko.

Motodachi-geiko

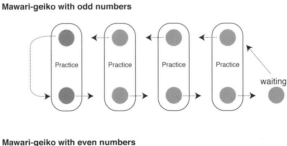

Mawari-geiko with odd numbers

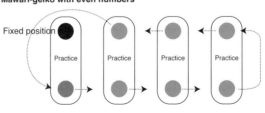

Mawari-geiko with even numbers

Motodachi

Whether acting as a dedicated motodachi or taking turns in mawari geiko, motodachi's job is to enable kakarite to practice technique correctly in the best timing and distance for his or her level. For kirikaeshi, uchikomi geiko, kakarigeiko, or waza geiko, motodachi should dictate the opportunity, making clear sharp openings for kakarite to attack.

It is impossible to do this without maintaining strong mind contact and building up pressure between you and the attacker. Only when you are in tune with each other should you give openings for your opponent to strike. These should be obvious and consistent but subtle. Move the shinai point to the right to receive men and to the left for kote. Raise the shinai for dou.

Timing is crucial. Do not stand around showing a target when kakarite is out of distance. Meet his shinai pressure with stronger pressure and open quickly as he reaches distance or makes seme. If you are acting as motodachi for a partner trying oji-waza, you should attack with total commitment. A lazy motodachi is no fun to practice with. Unless you give it 100 percent, kakarite soon loses momentum.

One of the biggest challenges for motodachi is knowing how hard to stretch an opponent in kakarigeiko. In this situation the receiver can throw in countless variables, escalating the practice from being a mere target, to employing oji-waza and ai-uchi, making tai-atari, through to breaking technique and posture by knocking down the shinai at the point of attack.

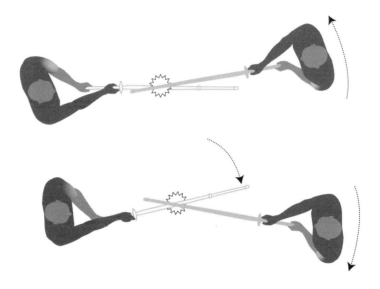

All of these are valid and useful when used appropriately. The key is that you should aim to encourage and not destroy kakarite's kendo. This may sound contradictory, but treatment that would confuse and deflate a less experience player will normally make a more experienced kendoka stronger and more determined.

Kirikaeshi

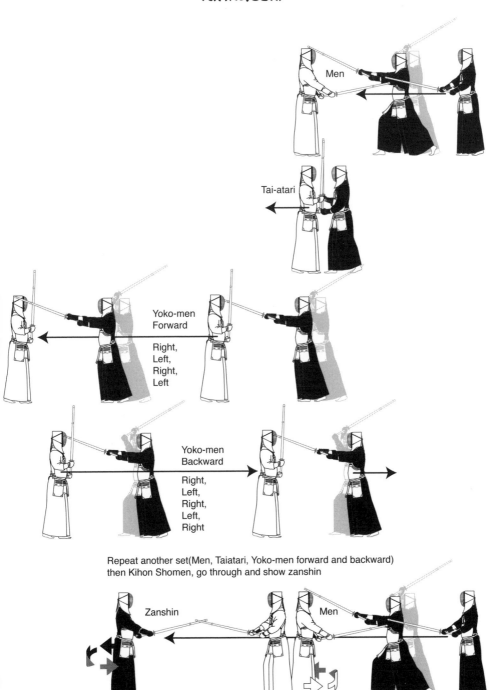

Men

Tai-atari

Yoko-men
Forward

Right,
Left,
Right,
Left

Yoko-men
Backward

Right,
Left,
Right,
Left,
Right

Repeat another set(Men, Taiatari, Yoko-men forward and backward)
then Kihon Shomen, go through and show zanshin

Zanshin

Men

Kirikaeshi, sometimes called uchi kaeshi, is one of the most beneficial kendo training exercises. It helps improve cutting, footwork, breathing, and kiai and most importantly the union of all of these in ki-ken-tai-itchi. It can be practiced as a kihon drill or at the beginning or end (sometimes both) of keiko with your instructor.

The normal sequence for kirikaeshi is a strike to shomen followed by four yoko-men cuts going forward and then by five yoko men attacks going back, with the pattern repeated before moving through with a final shomen attack. This is usual but, by no means the only method; with various permutations of cuts backwards and forwards being equally acceptable. In fact kirikaeshi can be adapted to match the space available and is sometimes conducted up and down the length of the dojo. Kirikaeshi can also be adapted to practice dou uchi or a mixture of dou and men strikes.

Whatever the format, the elements of kirikaeshi should remain the same. You should start from issoku-ito-ma. Some teachers suggest stepping back to adjust distance. Personally I am not a fan of this, as stepping back weakens your approach and intention. From Issoku-ito-ma, you should step into your own cutting distance, lifting your left hand up above your mengane to strike a correct kihon shomen; paying attention to ki-ken-tai-itchi.

There are two schools of thought on the next step. One suggests that you should make firm tai-atari before motodachi receives the sequence of yoko men attacks. The other requires you to just gently touch mototodachi as the signal for him to move back. I would suggest this latter approach for less experienced players, as you do not need to worry about applying power to make body contact, but can instead concentrate on striking yoko men correctly.

Always start by striking to the right and also ensure that you lift your left hand above the mengane as for shomen. There is a tendency among beginners to try to hit quickly by not lifting the shinai sufficiently. This must be resisted, as must the desire to hit quickly with the hands if your foot and body movement is not equally fast. It is also tempting to bounce or jump with both feet in a fixed position. This is also a no-no, with the imperative being on correct footwork, with the back foot coming into position at the same moment as you make the strike.

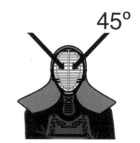

The cut itself should be at 45 degrees, so that you hit between the 3rd and 5th mengane. The shinai should be raised straight through your center, using relaxed hands to guide the hasuji to the target.

Kiai and breathing are important. You should fill up with air, letting some out in your kakegoe while in to-ma and then aim to breathe out continuously through the first shomen, the next 9 yokomen, and the final shomen. So the sequence should be ya – men – men, men, men, men, men, men, men, men, men – men; in one breath. This is followed by a quick intake of air and then repeat.

When you return from the final yoko-men to starting distance you should take pains to do so in suriashi (backwards of course), do not cross your feet.

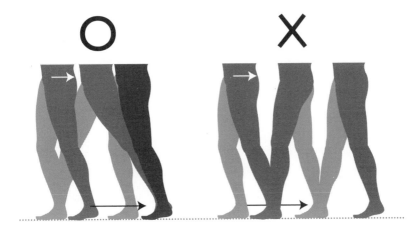

On the final shomen, motodachi should step to the side and you should go through to safe distance with good zanshin. For motodachi, it is important that you receive the cut as close as possible to your own men allowing kakarite to aim correctly rather than stopping the cut to hit your shinai. You should also try to receive with the shinai to the opposite side to your leading foot.

Uchikomi Geiko

Meaning striking practice, uchikomi geiko is where kakarite strikes targets shown by motodachi. These can be in random order with motodachi deciding on which opening he will make as kakarite moves into issoku ito maai, or attacks can be practiced in a pre-arranged pattern. One commonly used sequence is men, kote, dou, kote-men, kote-dou, men. Whether following a fixed pattern or responding to given opportunities, uchikomi geiko should be sustained and concentrated. Kakarite's objective is to make these strikes accurately while maintaining good posture and form. After each strike motodachi moves out of kakarite's path allowing him to make correct zanshin and to go through to safe distance.

Start from close distance

Bad posture

After striking, kakarite should take three steps past motodachi and turn right and step forward into toi maai. This pre-arranged approach is sometimes referred to as yakusoku geiko.

for Men   for Kote   for Do

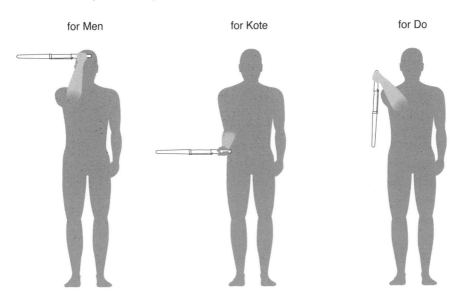

Uchikomi geiko can also be practiced against a partner holding an uchiko-mi-bo or shinai to simulate a target. This is a good way for new beginners to learn about distance and correct cutting without administering too many headaches.

Kakarigeiko

Kakarigeiko on the other hand requires motodachi to stay in chudan, forcing kakarite to make his or her own openings. Kakarigeiko calls for rapid, continuous attacks and if done correctly, cannot be sustained for much more than 30 seconds to a minute.

Motodachi's role in kakarigeiko is to allow only effective strikes to hit. This can be done just by maintaining and relaxing kamae, or by taking a more proactive stance by punishing unsuccessful attacks. You may use harai or osae techniques to knock or push an attacker's shinai down, or to the side. This treatment can be ratcheted up by the use of tai sabaki (moving the body out of line) as kakarite attempts to strike, or by responding to some of the attacks with oji waza. Other options are the introduction of taiatari (butsukarigeiko) and the ultimate tactic of responding with full-on attacks, turning the practice into aikakarigeiko.

Kakarigeiko is an important practice which increases speed, fluidity, and attacking spirit. It is only by training in this "see it, hit it" fashion that you teach yourself not to consciously think about attacking, but to respond instantly to opportunities.

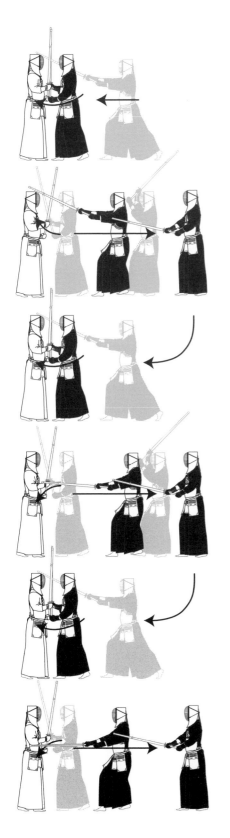

Butsukarigeiko

Butsukarigeiko is effectively taiatari practice. It can be incorporated into kakarigeiko or performed as a separate exercise. In this case kakarite makes a shomen attack to motodachi who stands his ground as kakarite comes forward and resists his movement with his body. Both parties should drop their hands to navel height and push down with their hands while pushing their hips forward with the left foot.

Then as both adjust to correct tsubazeriai position, kakarite steps back to execute hiki waza, as previously described.

Yakusoku Geiko

Yakusoku geiko is the term used to describe the practice of pre-arranged techniques. It is however a fairly broad catch all term covering a number of training methods. It could describe uchikomi geiko or waza geiko or even hikitategeiko where one or both parties set themselves the objective of successfully using a certain technique during the keiko.

Waza geiko

Waza geiko generally refers to any training exercise used to learn or improve specific kendo techniques. Many kendo teachers have developed their own drills to ensure that students grasp the most important elements of each waza. The list of drills that follow is just a sample and is meant to give you a flavor of how techniques can be practiced. The most common form of waza geiko is for a technique to be repeated in the form in which to use it. Usually waza geiko training is done with partners of similar grade, often as mawari geiko so that you can experiment with people of different physical types.

Shikake Waza Geiko

Men uchi

Working as a pair, both partners take turns to strike men. This can done on a one for one basis or with each partner repeating the strike a number of pre-arranged times and then changing.

1. Starting in close distance, you strike your opponent's men without moving the position of your feet. Ensuring that your posture is correct and that your left heel is off the ground, swing your shinai up to jodan position and down to strike your opponent's men. You should ensure that your shinai maintains a central path and that your shoulders, elbows, and wrists are relaxed making correct tenouchi after you strike the target. You should ensure that you use the muscles of your waist and back as you strike. Also ensure that you raise and lower the shinai in one action.

2. Move back to Issoku ito ma and make the same men strike, this time pushing off from your left foot as you raise the shinai and slide your right foot forward bringing your left foot up so the toes line up with right heel as you strike. Again your shoulder and arm action should be relaxed and the power of your left leg should be added to that of your back muscles. Ensuring that you hit shomen correctly with your shinai's datotsu bu, you should stop "on the spot" in front of your partner without continuing your forward motion.

3. Starting in toi maai, you step forward into issoku ito distance, making seme by pushing in with strong chudan. As you reach position, push off with your left foot, raising the shinai as you throw your right foot forward. Keeping your front foot parallel with the ground swing the shinai down to strike men as you make a fumikomi stamp with the right foot, immediately bringing the left foot up to position. Stop instantly in front of your opponent on making contact with the target. Do not allow your forward motion to continue.

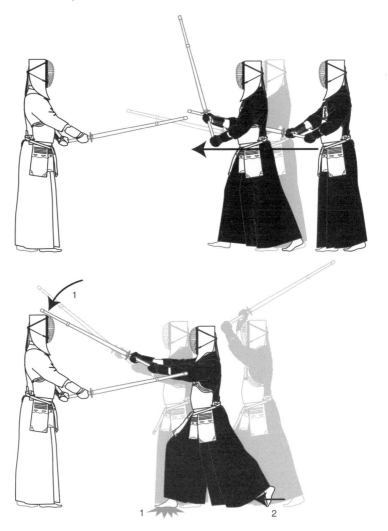

4. Again from toi maai, step forward into issoku ito maai making seme. As before, push off with your left foot, raising the shinai as you throw

your right foot forward. Swing the shinai down to strike men as you make a fumikomi stamp with the right foot and this time as your left foot comes up, you continue into zanshin (keeping the point of the shinai at your opponent's men height) and keep going in a straight line for three steps, turning right into chudan and step forward.

The idea of this drill is to start with the fundamental principles of relaxing your shoulders and arms and using your body to cut strongly. It teaches you correct posture and balance, as the ability to stop or go at will is essential to smooth controlled kendo. It should also help you build kiai as you build towards the final attack, which we approach with total commitment as we accelerate into zanshin.

Kote uchi

This drill is similar to that used for men-uchi, but this time we factor in the differences required to achieve correct distance and to make appropriate seme.

1. From chikai maai, lift your shinai just above your eye line and strike without moving. Ensure that you strike kote sharply and correctly as

badly executed kote can result in pain and injury over the course of extended kihon drills.

2. From issoku ito maai slide in with your right foot as you lift the shinai and bring up the right foot as you strike.

3. Do not continue forward. Remember that kote is a smaller technique than men, so there is a need to move your hands slightly ahead of your feet. Also remember to move your right foot over diagonally so that it is in line with motodachi's right foot and you are square on to the target.

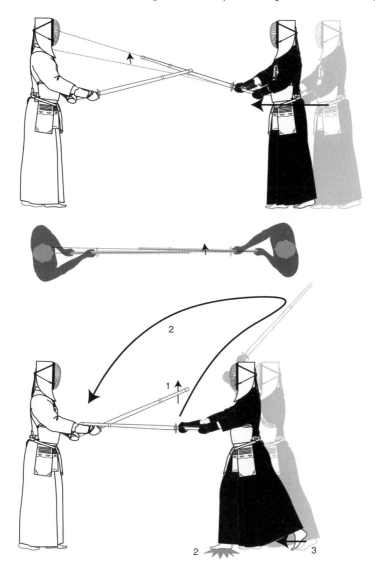

Move to toi maai. Step in as described for men but as you do so raise the point of your shinai slightly to the right towards motodachi's left eye. This should make him believe that he has the chance to strike men and he raises his right kote slightly, showing the target. Making a controlled fumikomi step and hikitsuke, strike kote sharply and stop on the spot.

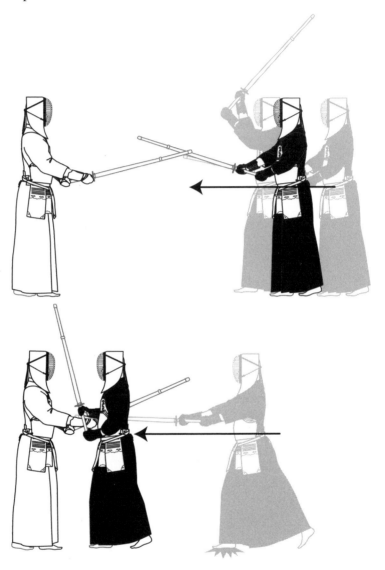

4. Repeat step 4, but continue forward stopping in tsubazeriai.

Dou uchi

Dou requires particular attention to distance and hasuji (angle of the blade). A similar drill to the one just described for kote can be used.

1. Strike from in front of your opponent in close distance without moving forward, using your back muscles.

2. Strike using sliding footwork stopping in front of your opponent.

3. Strike using fumikomi footwork stopping in front of your opponent.

4. Strike using fumikomi footwork and then continue your movement diagonally to the right (opponent's left side), after you complete the strike, either shortening your grip or releasing your right hand from the tsuka.

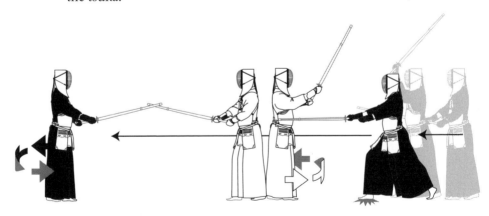

5. Taking three steps through turn to face your opponent.

The key points to focus on are:

- Ensure that the cut is made in a downward motion (not from side to side)

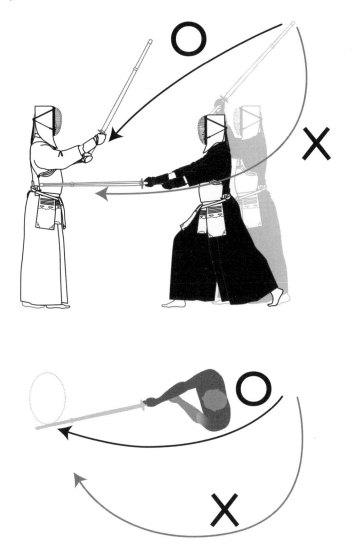

- Strike while directly in front of your partner, not as you move diagonally

- Ensure that you hit the left side of the dou with the correct part of the shinai

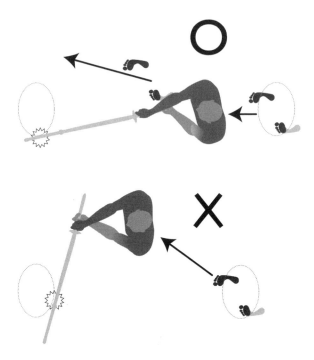

- Turn your wrists so that you strike with bottom slat of the shinai

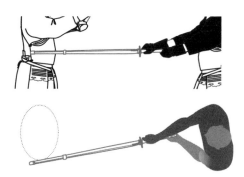

- Remember, move through to the right after hitting the target, not before
- Keep watching your opponent as you move through to zanshin.

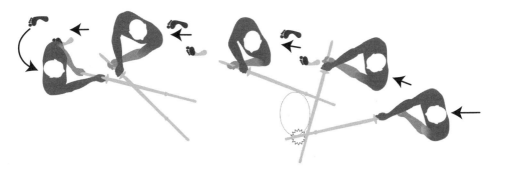

There are numerous variations on how dou can be practiced. For example, it can be done with ayumi-ashi (walking footwork) as in kendo no kata no 7, or you can step to the left and strike so that you pass in a straight line on your opponent's right hand side.

Ayumi-ashi

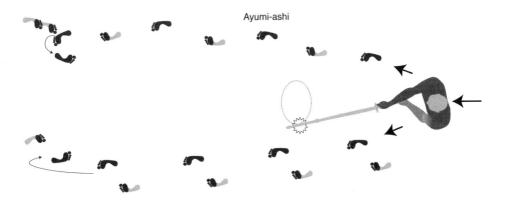

Oji Waza Geiko

Oji waza certainly benefits from practice in this drill form. It allows you to work on seme and timing while developing the basic technique. Waza can be broken down into component parts, as per the shikake waza drills already described. For example, with kaeshi waza, the block and strike can be practiced in close distance and then as the technique takes shape, you can lengthen the distance and add seme and zanshin. Again, I have included just a sample of the drills that can be used to improve oji waza.

Men suriage men

If your timing and distance are correct, you can just push off from your left foot as your opponent makes his attack, lift your shinai up as his comes down and just deflect his blow with the shape of your shinai before striking men. Keep in mind that suriage translates as "sliding lift" and is not harai waza. To practice this technique:

1. Motodachi and kakarite start in issoku ito distance and motodachi makes a repeated swing to kakarite's men without stepping forward.

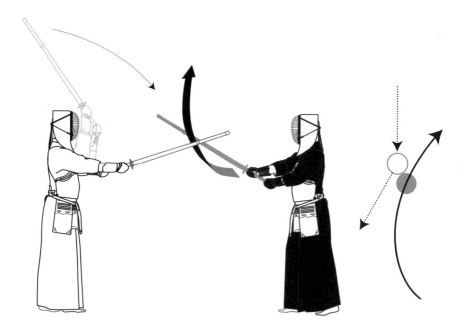

Kakarite repeatedly attempts the suriage lift against motodachi's men strike until he is confident that it is working well, without completing the down stroke or moving his feet.

2. In the same distance he completes the up-down motion, striking motodachi's men as he makes a small step forward.

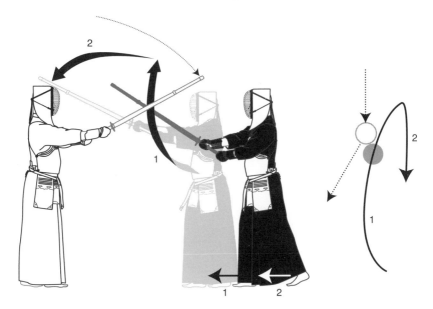

3. He then returns to toi maai and steps forward to issoku ito distance, lifting the point of his shinai to the right (motodachi's left eye), forcing him to attack men.

4. As he does so, kakarite raises the shinai up in the suriage movement and cuts down to men while stepping forward with fumikomi ashi. He should instantly bring his left foot up in hikitsuke. At this point

motodachi should step to the right allowing kakarite to take three steps forward before turning to face him and repeating the exercise.

The key factors to success are:

- You have to keep the point of your shinai forward

- You must not anticipate your opponent's attack, but you should relax and wait until it is nearly complete
- Distance must be correct, so that the suriage is made by the monouchi touching the monouchi
- Your opponent must attack correctly, lifting and cutting down in a single movement and maintaining the center line

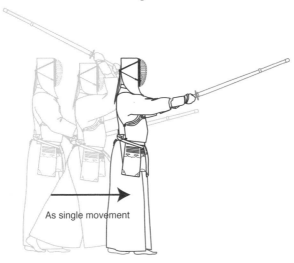

As single movement

- If this is not possible, then a good alternative kihon drill is to make your opponent attack tsuki and respond with suriage men

- Just use gentle pressure to slide your shinai up against his. Do not put power into your right hand. Some teachers suggest making a "D" shaped movement to deflect the shinai. I think that this is overkill and requires too much right hand pressure. A simple slide upward should be enough.

Once you have made a successful strike, you should continue forward, through your opponent's center line, maintaining zanshin, and turning when you are in safe distance.

Kote suriage men

For suriage against kote, there are some marked changes. First you need to move your left foot out diagonally while pushing your left hand forward and turning your right wrist counterclockwise.

This makes the suriage sharper and into more of a blocking motion. Your kote is closer to your opponent than your men, so the suriage should be made closer to your tsuba. Although this is a "harder" technique than men suriage men, again do not be tempted to use too much right hand power.

1. Both partners stand in issoku ito distance in chudan kamae. Motodachi makes a pre-agreed number of kote strikes. Kakarite responds to each by stepping diagonally to the left with his left foot and by pushing his shinai forward while turning his wrists counterclockwise against the shinogi of motodachi's descending shinai, breaking the trajectory towards kote.

As the two shinai make contact, kakarite's right foot also moves diagonally to the left leaving him standing to motodachi's right in correct kendo foot position.

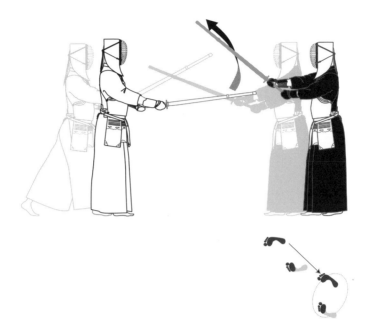

2. After this has been successfully accomplished a number of times, repeat the exercise, this time with kakarite continuing the shinai movement upwards so that his left hand is in line with his own dou mune. As the shinai moves upwards he pushes forward from the left foot and strikes shomen in a smooth downward motion. Bring the right foot up and make hikitsuke as you complete the strike.

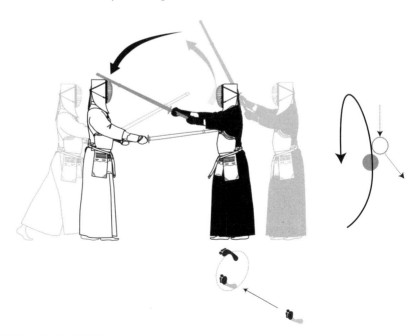

3. Finally repeat the process at full speed with fumikomi ashi going through into zanshin and turning back into distance.

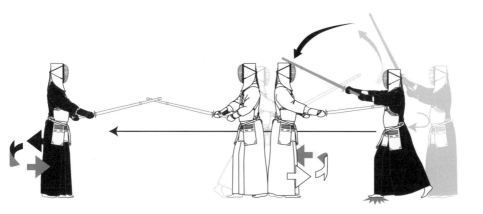

Men kaeshi dou

1. Start the drill standing close enough to each other to hit without moving. Motodachi delivers a series of men strikes to kakarite while both remain in the same position. Kakarite raises his shinai, pushing the point forward and blocking the attack on the shinai's omote side, turns his hands to strike dou in one continuous up and down movement.

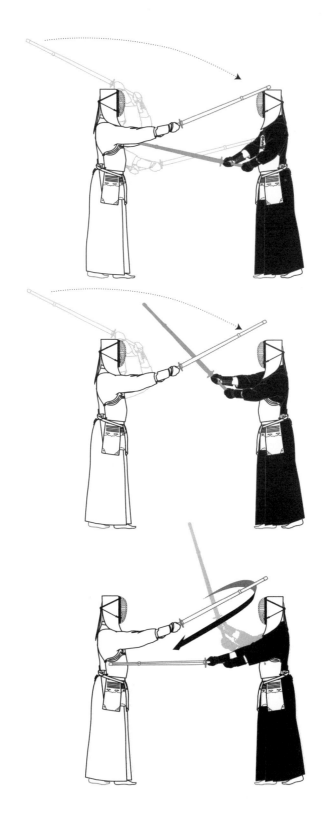

2. The process is repeated from issoku ito ma with kakarite moving the right foot forward as he blocks the men strike and the left foot being quickly pulled toes level with right heel as he strikes dou.

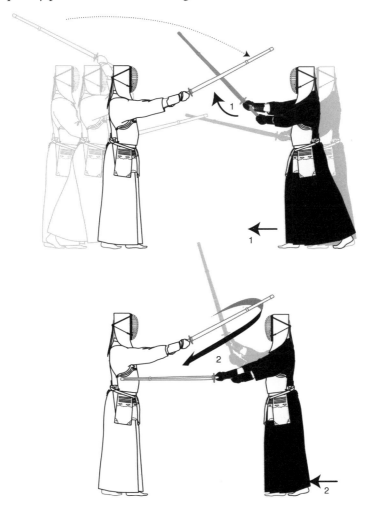

3. The process is repeated, this time with kakarite moving diagonally to the right (motodachi's left), into zanshin after striking dou.

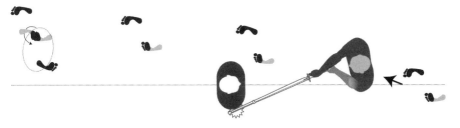

4. As you move through, either slide your left hand up the tsuka or release it completely.

Slide   Open

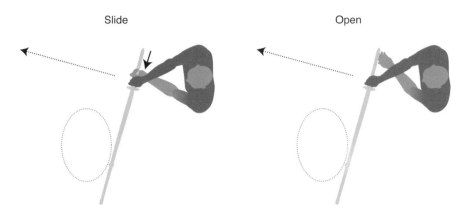

Key points:

- Make sure that you approach the technique with an attacking mind! Do not wait for your opponent to strike men and then react

- Ensure your posture is correct but with your balance just slightly forward

- The block and strike should be one smooth, continuous movement

- As with all oji waza, make sure the point of your shinai is going forward rather than lifting up and back
- Hit dou while you are in front of your opponent and then move diagonally for your zanshin, do not hit after you have moved
- Keep your left hand in the center and only break your right hand grip as you move diagonally
- Make sure you hit the side of the dou and do not just scrape across the front
- Have correct hasuji; the bottom *take* should make full contact with the dou
- Keep correct distance so that you hit with the datotsu bu.

Hasuji

All of these elements are important, but in my view, attacking mind is the most significant, pull your opponent in and make him attack in your space and timing.

Men nuki dou

Nuki dou requires different timing and distance to that used for kaeshi dou. Whereas with kaeshi dou you are responding to motodachi's men in close distance as his strike is close to completion, with nuki dou you are striking dou as you step out of distance while motodachi's shinai is still raised in the furikaburi (swing up) position. The close distance preparation described for some of the other oji techniques therefore is not of value for nuki dou and you should start the technique in issoku ito maai.

1. Starting from issoku ito maai, raise the point of your shinai to moto-dachi's left eye to encourage him to attack men. Motodachi should

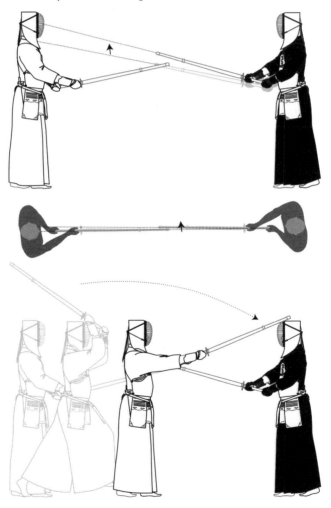

respond by stepping in and hitting men. This action should be repeated three times.

2. On the third strike from motodachi, as he makes his upswing, push from the left foot and slide your right foot diagonally to your right while raising your shinai. Then strike dou as you draw up your left foot. Make sure that you strike correctly cutting down and bringing your hands forward while rotating your wrists counterclockwise so as to make full contact with the target. As mentioned before, you have the choice of sliding your left hand up the tsuka as you strike or you can release your left hand after you strike to allow your forward diagonal movement to continue.

3. After several successful repetitions of the dou strike, add zanshin by moving through with okuri ashi footwork, turning to face motodachi when in safe distance.

This technique can also be done using ayumi ashi footwork as in Nihon kendo no kata number 7. In this case, you cross your feet so that the left foot leads. At the point of striking and you continue through to zanshin with ayumi ashi.

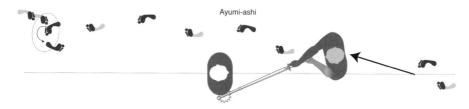

Ayumi-ashi

Men kaeshi men

The perfect drill for men kaeshi men is kirikaeshi. Another less energy intensive approach is to stand in issoku ito maai with a partner.

1. Motodachi should then make a succession of continuous shomen strikes from a standing position without stopping or changing the rhythm.

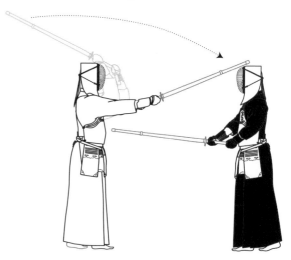

2. Kakarite responds by blocking the shinai on omote and striking mo-todachi's right yoko men in hiraki ashi footwork with the left foot leading.

3. He then blocks to the ura side and attacks left yoko men in hiraki ashi with the right foot leading.

4. Motodachi then repeats the men strike process, but now does so moving forward and back using okuri ashi footwork.

5. Kakarite responds as before, this time increasing the size of his hiraki ashi steps to be in correct striking distance.

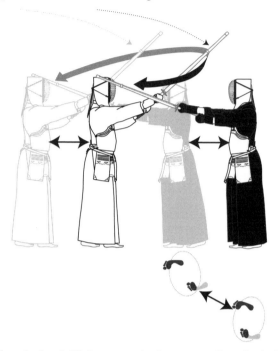

6. Finally break the drill down to single men strikes for kakarite to practice completing the technique through to zanshin. Zanshin takes the form of stepping back into chudan kamae.

Kote nuki men

1. Both partners stand in issoku ito distance in chudan kamae. Motoda-chi makes a pre-agreed number of kote strikes. Kakarite responds to each by stepping back and pushing his shinai forward and up so that the right kote moves up to men height, out of the path of motodachi's shinai, just before the point of impact. He then returns to distance and the process is repeated.

2. When you are satisfied that you are able to do this easily, resume the drill, this time striking down to hit motodachi's men on the return step forward. Stop after hitting and step back into distance.

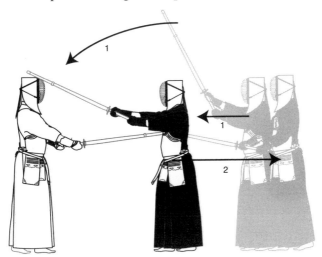

3. Finally repeat the process going through into zanshin and turning back into safe distance.

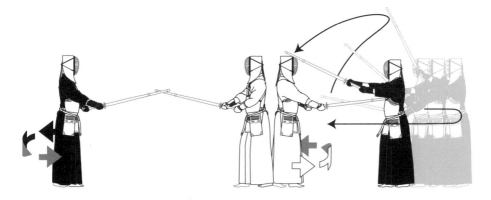

| CHAPTER 4: WAZA GEIKO

Jigeiko

Many people see jigeiko as the more valuable and enjoyable part of kendo and that if in the early stages of our kendo careers we do enough nasty kihon geiko, we eventually graduate and qualify to enjoy practices that consist entirely of jigeiko. This is not the case. Jigeiko is no more important than any other element of training and it needs to be undertaken with the same level of dedication, energy, and enthusiasm as any other form of keiko.

It is worth considering the meaning of kendo terms for training methods. The generic "keiko" has the connotation of "thinking or reflecting on the past" and is used in budo and other traditional Japanese arts. The word renshu means repeated practice and can be used for any sport as can torainingu. Jigeiko in kendo applies to free practice, but this can be broken down more precisely to gokakugeiko, meaning practice between people of the same level and hikitate geiko or practice between senior and junior.

In both of these forms it is imperative that they be approached with full spirit and concentration which remains engaged from beginning to end. The keiko starts with the initial bow to each other and finishes with the final bow. For this reason keiko should not be overly long, as it is difficult to remain constantly engaged and ready to attack for longer than five minutes. The intensity with which you should approach jigeiko also dictates that talking should be kept to a necessary minimum, with advice kept for discussion after practice.

Gokakugeiko

Gokakugeiko is jigeiko practiced between those of similar grade. You should keep in mind that this is training to improve and develop your technique and that each waza should be delivered to the very best of your ability. You should not rely on incorrect technique to help the success of an attack, neither should you block without the intention of returning a strike purely to avoid being hit. Instead your actions should be honest and in the spirit of kendo.

As you stand up from sonkyo you should try to meet your opponent's mind, this is referred to as tachiai, a term meaning "standing and meeting" that is also used to describe high grade demonstration matches because of the level of focus, verging on telepathy, involved. Do not rush in, but settle your breathing and establish your presence with a big kiai before trying your opponent's kamae with the point of your shinai. Your objective is to take shodachi (the first point), so you need to find an opening, break your opponent's center, or induce him to attack so that you can respond with an oji waza.

Once shodachi has been taken, by either of you, you should immediately re-establish "mind contact" and continue to the next point. You should accept points made against you with a generous spirit, but not spend overly long in acknowledging them. Instead keep your mind level and concentrate on the next opportunity.

This is an opportunity to polish your technique against opponents of different physical types and kendo styles, so it helps you to establish which techniques work in which circumstances. It is important however to constantly experiment with new techniques and timing. If you constantly rely on a few favorite waza, you become lazy and predictable.

Hikitategeiko

Hikitategeiko is the practice of jigeiko between partners of unequal grade, so it is best described from the perspectives of kakarite and motodachi. The important thing to remember is that you start as equals and you should approach the keiko with a 50:50 attitude. The less experienced exponent is tasked with making shodachi or first point. Once that has or has not been achieved, the relationship reverts to that of student and teacher.

Kakarite

As already stated, you should display tenacity and confidence with the aim of taking the first point. As in gokakugeiko you need to challenge motodachi's center either breaking his kamae to make an opportunity or force him to attack and react with your own technique. Motodachi may genuinely lose to this challenge, or decide that your technique deserves to be acknowledged and let you through his defence. He may also decide to assert his own technique and beat you to shodachi.

Whatever the outcome, you should continue to aggressively attack. In situations where there is an obvious gap in grades, kakarite should concentrate on trying shikake waza rather than expecting motodachi to fall for an oji waza trap. Work on breaking the center and approach with correct posture, distance, and footwork. It may well be that motodachi identifies an error in your technique and the keiko changes into uchikomi geiko or kakarigeiko. This is not an unusual situation, so respond to the signals he gives you and give it your all.

There is a school of thought that says that it is better for someone at ikkyu or shodan level to practice with opponents who are only one or two dan grades higher, rather than waste the time of an eighth dan. I personally disagree with this philosophy, as the high grade teachers in question normally have a unique ability to spot your mistakes and to hand you an instant remedy to fix them.

Motodachi

Motodachi's role is to stretch kakarite without demoralizing him. As such you are advised to pitch your keiko level at half a dan grade to a dan grade above that of your opponent. This is not always possible, but you get the general idea.

Motodachi should of course aim to keep control of timing and distance, allowing good techniques to strike and refusing unsuccessful attacks. He should also ensure that the keiko is conducted safely and that kakarite is not in danger of bumping into other players or obstacles in the dojo.

Motodachi can of course work on his own technique during hikitategeiko. As well as the obvious opportunities to try oji-waza, he should conduct each exercise with full spirit constantly thinking about seme, whether using it to make his own shikake waza or relaxing the pressure to allow kakarite to attack.

Organizing jigeiko

Gokakugeiko can be practiced in mawari-geiko or by individual request with the more senior (no matter by how little) of the two kendoka taking the senior position in kamiza.

Hikitategeiko usually takes place with instructors or seniors arranged in grade order on the kamiza side of the dojo. Typically those who start the session sitting on the kamiza side, continue in kamiza throughout the practice, with the more senior students moving from shimoza to kamiza for individual keiko if requested.

Students are normally expected to wait in line to practice with instructors. Ideally this should be kept to a queue of three or four people at a time for each teacher. This is not always possible and at some dojo or at special practices in Japan, I have seen people wait for an hour to practice with a particularly famous sensei.

Teachers therefore have far less rest time in each practice session than the students that practice with them. It is expected that students give 100 percent to balance the equation.

Shidogeiko

Most kendo teachers mix other forms of keiko into the jigeiko session. A typical practice could look like one of the following:

1. Kakarite starts with kirikaeshi, then moves on to hikitategeiko. Motodachi then challenges kakarite to ippon shobu (one-point match) before a brief kakarigeiko.

2. Both parties fight to take shodachi (first point), before motodachi increases the opportunities for attack in hikitategeiko then finishes with kakarigeiko or kirikaeshi.

Kata Geiko

I do not intend to deal with kata in detail in this guide, as there are several good books and DVDs already available on the subject and frankly, kata deserves a lot more focus. Suffice it to say that kata incorporates all the principles and techniques of kendo into one structure and should be studied throughout your kendo career and not just frantically revised before grading examinations. It should be regularly incorporated into training sessions.

The term kata geiko can refer to the normal practice of kata, it can also be applied to training sessions that take the principles of particular kata and work on them in different formats either using bokuto or shinai. For example ippon me or the first form of the Tachi-no-kata teaches the timing, opportunity, and technique for men nuki men. This can be practiced in the following way:

As in kendo-no kata both players initially practice these movements without wearing bogu and use bokuto. Instead of taking the five steps from the formal start position into distance. The two opponents face each other in issoku-ito-maai. Uchidachi assumes the left jodan position, with his left foot forward and shidachi takes right jodan. Uchidachi (the attacker and senior partner) steps into cutting distance on the right foot in ayumi-ashi footwork and makes a big swing to men, stopping the monouchi of the bokuto di-

rectly above shidachi's left hand. He returns to the original position and repeats the action twice more.

On the third attempt, shidachi steps back, while moving the left foot and then the right while pulling his hands back out of the path of uchidachi's strike. He then steps forward on the right foot and draws his left foot up as he strikes uchidachi's men.

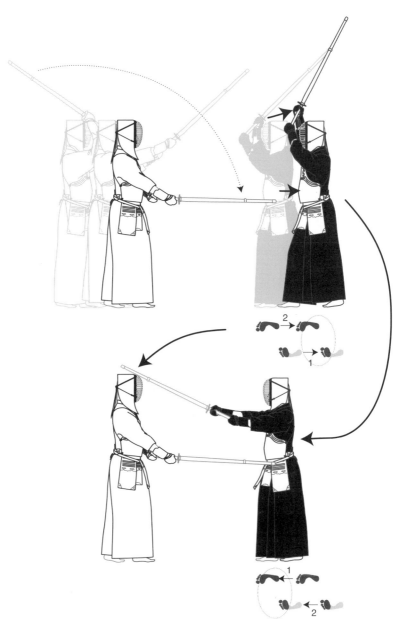

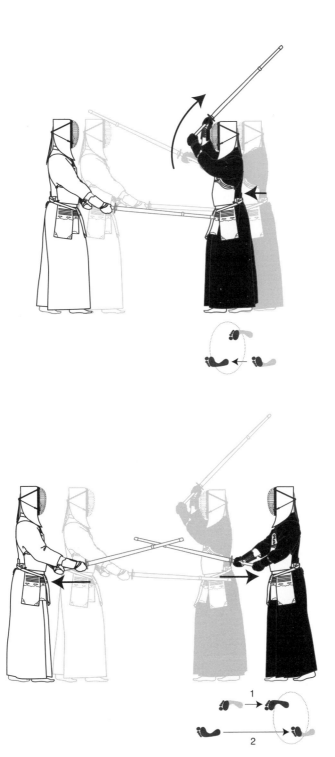

The exercise then continues into zanshin with shidachi following through into left jodan while advancing the left foot . He then returns to chudan, returning the left foot to its normal position. Uchidachi takes a small step back moving the left foot first as shidachi takes jodan and repeats the action as he returns to chudan. Both partners then return to the starting position and repeat the sequence with both taking turns as uchidachi and shidachi. The sequence can then be repeated wearing bogu and using shinai.

All seven forms of the Tachi-no-kata, (long sword) kata can be practiced in this way. While kendo-no-kata must be practiced in its original form, this is a useful way to translate the riai (purpose) of the kata into shinai kendo.

CHAPTER 5

Structuring a kendo session

The way that a kendo session is structured depends on the time allotted to it and the level of students taking part. Some suggested lesson plans are as follows.

2 hour session

1. 5 minutes warming up exercises
2. 5 minutes suburi
3. 10 minutes kirikaeshi
4. 10 minutes uchikomi geiko
5. 30 minutes waza geiko (demonstration and practice)
6. 5 minutes break
7. 40 minutes jigeiko
8. 10 minutes kakarigeiko
9. 5 minutes cool down

2 hour session version 2

1. 5 minutes warming up exercises
2. 30 minutes kata geiko
3. 30 minutes waza geiko (based on kata techniques)
4. 5 minutes break
5. 40 minutes jigeiko
6. 10 minutes kakarigeiko
7. 5 minutes cool down

1 hour session

1. 5 minutes warm up
2. 5 minutes suburi
3. 10 minutes kirikaeshi
4. 10 minutes uchikomi geiko
5. 25 minutes jigeiko
6. 5 minutes cool down

Other Structures

Mixed mawari geiko

My favorite approach is to take mawari geiko and combine kihon practice and jigeiko. So for the first three or four practices everyone starts with kirikaeshi then moves on to a short jigeiko with the same partner. After each we change partners and move through repetitions of waza geiko, transitioning to jigeiko with each opponent. So a one hour session would include kirikaeshi/jigeiko, men uchikomi/jigeiko, kote uchikomi/jigeiko, dou uchikomi/jigeiko and then on to combining ni-dan waza and finally uchikomi geiko and kakarigeiko. In this way, as well as including basic practice, we are thinking about using correct technique in the jigeiko sessions.

Senior grade practice

On occasions when senior grade kendoka are together for meeting or seminars or when they are together to spend time with high grade visitors it is difficult for them to find time to practice together. One way to overcome this is to have seniors and visitors enjoy a brief mawari geiko for 10 or 15 minutes While more junior students watch and then for the seniors to return to motodachi position for open keiko for the remainder of the session.

Godogeiko

These are normally special open practices where kendoka have the chance to practice hikitategeiko with senior instructors. Examples of these are the monthly ZNKR Godogeiko at the Tokyo Budokan or morning practice at the Kyoto Takai.

Warm up and cool down exercises

Before we begin a kendo session we need to ensure that we warm up and stretch to avoid damaging muscles by making strenuous movements from a cold start. Kendo puts particular strain on the legs so there is possibility of achilles tendon and calf muscle injuries should you not warm up. A typical warm up session may take the following form. Stretching exercises should be done slowly, holding for a count of six. Typically these exercises should be repeated four to six times, two to three times each side.

1. Jog around the dojo for two or three minutes before returning to your original position.
2. With feet apart reach down and touch the floor then stretch up above your head, going onto tip-toes.

3. In the same position reach down and then around to the side and then above your head in a circular motion, alternating direction.

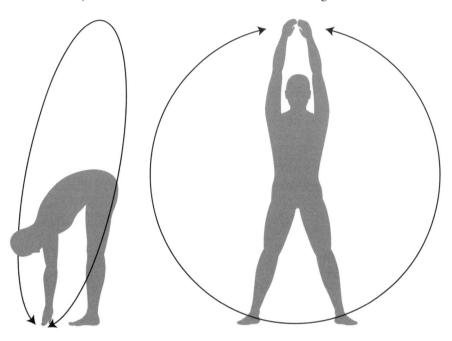

4. Put your hands on your hips and rotate them in a circular motion, regularly changing direction.

5. Reach behind you on alternate sides throwing your leading arm up at a 45 degree angle, ensuring that your heels are off the ground and that you pivot on the balls of your feet.

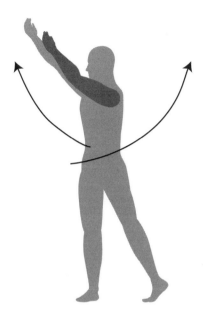

6. Alternate stretching your arms across your chest and placing them in the crook of your other arm, completing the stretch by pulling back with the forearm.

7. Alternating arms push your upper arm up so that it is perpendicular with the side of your head then hold the elbow with the opposing hand and pull across behind your head.

8. Rotate wrists, frequently changing direction.

9. Stretch fingers out and pull back in by opening and closing your fists.

10. Push your chin down and turn your head alternately from left to right etc.

11. Move your whole head around in a circle frequently changing direction. Ensure that you do not let your chin point up as your head circles backwards.

12. Stand on one leg holding the ankle in one hand and rotate the foot, holding the toes with the other hand. Change direction and leg.

13. With both feet together bend the knees and rotate, holding your hands on the kneecaps, change direction.

14. Standing flat on one foot with your knee bent, extend the other leg forward with the heel touching the floor. Place both hands on the bent knee and stretch the calf muscle of the extended leg, alternating legs.

15. Squat on one leg extending the other to the side so that it rests on the inside edge of the foot. Stabilize your balance by placing both hands in front of you on the floor. Push your weight down and alternate legs.

16. Repeat this process but with toes of the extended leg pointing up so that you feel the stretch in your hamstring.

17. Start in kendo footwork but with both feet flat on the floor and widen your stance pushing down on your straight left leg to stretch your Achilles tendon. Change feet, progressively widening the gap between legs. You can also increase the tension by slightly bending the forward knee.

18. Complete the session by jumping on the spot.

This is by no means comprehensive and there are many other sequences and exercises that can be used. Very often in kendo we go through this warm up with the instructor or a senior student leading by counting through the exercise in Japanese with the other students responding. So for example the leader would call *ichi, ni, san, shi* and the students will respond *go, roku, shichi, hachi.*

An exercise sequence like this, minus the jogging and jumping, should be used at the end of a session as a cool down aid to help disperse lactic acid in the muscles, thus avoiding next day aches. In this case the exercises should be conducted in a calm quite fashion, perhaps minus the counting. Unfortunately very few dojo, including my own, do this as we invariably try to cram as much kendo as we can into the session.

Hitori Geiko

Hitori geiko is individual practice or methods used to practice without an opponent. In most cases these drills are conducted as a group in the dojo, but they can be used on occasions when you do not have the opportunity to train with others.

Suburi

Suburi is a vital part of ongoing kendo training. Its importance cannot be overstated in developing correct grip and cutting action.

In suburi we practice kendo technique by repeatedly hitting an imaginary opponent. Suburi is used to ensure that the path of the upswing and the strike are correct, that our hand and foot timing is coordinated, and that our posture and tenouchi is correct, as is our breathing and kiai. It is not a stamina exercise and should not be done at speeds that are too fast for you to control.

There are various schools of thought about how far back you should swing the shinai in preparation for the forward strike. Some teachers insist that the shinai should make contact with your buttocks, others say bring it no further back than the 45 degrees required for jodan kamae. Typically the type of suburi used can have a specific influence on your kendo, for instance bringing the shinai back in a large action can help correct shoulder movement while smaller technique will improve tenouchi and control.

Joge buri

Joge buri is the foundation stone of suburi. We start by raising the shinai in a big arc and then cutting through to a just below knee height, keeping the path of the shinai central to the center of our own body. As in all suburi from chudan position, the up and down swing should be continuous. The height to which we raise the shinai is open to debate. Some teachers suggest bringing the shinai back to touch your buttocks, with the objective of developing a relaxed shoulder movement, others recommend lifting the shinai to a 45 degree jodan position.

We should raise the shinai while in a static position with left heel off the ground, pushing forward from the left foot and then stepping out with the right foot in a sliding motion as the shinai moves through its arc. We complete the motion as the left foot is pulled into place with toes aligned to the right heel.

We then step backwards repeating the process with the shinai lifting as you start the step and reaching its final position as your right foot is pulled into place.

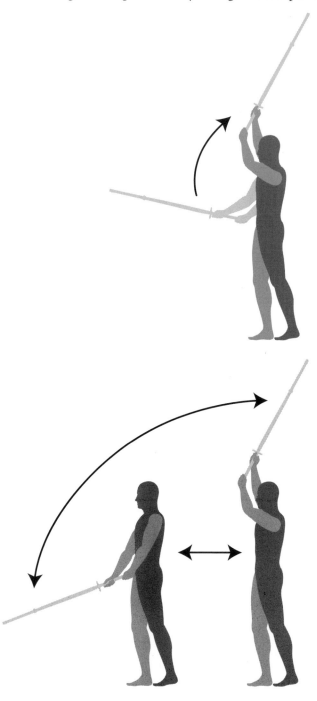

You should then continue striking as you alternate forward and backward foot movement. This becomes zenshin kotai joge buri.

Your grip on the shinai should be as described in the "holding the shinai" section, and you should pay particular attention to ensure that you do not open your left hand as the shinai is lifted over your head. Also while your grip should be relaxed, it should not be overly so to the point of not being able to stop the shinai's forward motion at the right point.

Naname buri

Naname buri follows an identical pattern, but this time with the shinai following a diagonal path, stopping in line alternately with your right and left knee. Footwork is forward and backward in a straight line as described for joge buri.

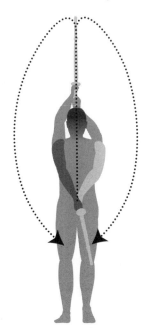

Shomen suburi

Shomen suburi consists of a series of single strikes to an imaginary opponent's shomen. You should use your own height as a guide to the level to which you deliver the strike. From a settled chudan kamae, push from your left foot raising your shinai to jodan position, i.e. 45 degrees straight back from the front of your head as the right foot starts to move forward and cut down to head height, finishing the strike as your left foot comes in line with your right heel. Ensure that your hands are relaxed and that your action consists of pushing up with your left hand and pulling up with your right then pull down with left hand and push forward with the right. This up down movement should be continuous without stopping between raising and striking. You should hit the imaginary target with relaxed hands and make tenouchi by gripping lightly as the shinai reaches jaw height.

As you complete the strike, deliberately pull your hands and shinai back into correct chudan kamae as you step back into your original position, ensuring that your balance and posture are correct before repeating the motion.

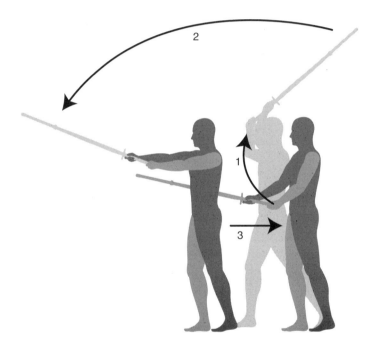

Zenshin kotai shomen suburi

Zenshin kotai shomen suburi is also known as double cutting or renzoku shomen suburi. This exercise teaches you to strike men as you advance and retreat. As in shomen suburi you must lift and strike in the "timing of one" and ensure that you start to move your feet and body in each direction before you lift the shinai.

You do not have the time to return to chudan between strikes, so you must ensure that you finish each with correct sae (snap) and tenouchi. It is far too easy to lapse into a comfortable rhythm where we are just swinging the shinai and not making distinct cuts with good posture. Remember every strike must count.

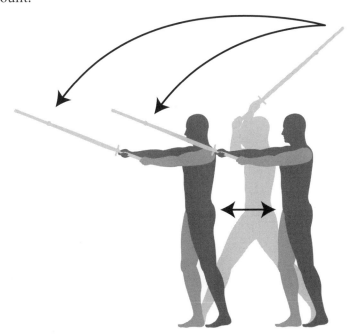

Yoko men suburi

Yoko men suburi is the preparation for kirikaeshi. Practiced as continuous strikes as with zenshin kotai shomen suburi, but this time to yoko men (the points at a 45 degree angle from the top of your imaginary opponent's men). This drill can be done stepping forwards and backwards or with hiraki ashi footwork, moving diagonally and alternating moving left and right foot forward. As well as ensuring that each strike is distinct, make sure that you continue to hit at the 45 degree point and do not make a horizontal strike.

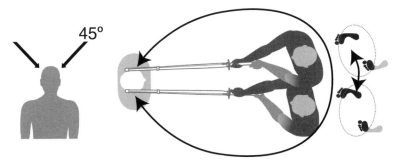

Dou suburi

Can be practiced as single strikes to the right dou with a diagonal step forward and back to chudan much in the same way as shomen suburi. It can also be practiced in the same way as yoko men suburi, striking to right and left dou in turn using hiraki ashi footwork. In both cases ensure that you turn your wrists so that the right thumb points outwards at the point of striking.

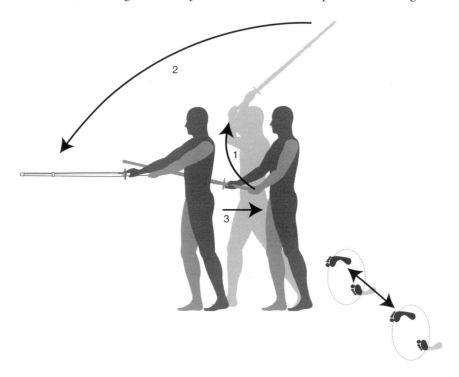

Choyaku suburi or hayasuburi

Sometimes incorrectly translated as jumping suburi, this exercise is the favorite of many Japanese high school clubs. It can be done either starting from jodan or chudan kamae and you should aim to repeatedly strike men as quickly as possible While stepping forward and back equally swiftly to maintain ki-ken-tai-ichi. Your whole body should move forward and back in correct posture and each strike to the men should be distinct and finish with correct sae. That is the theory. Hayasuburi are normally attempted with one continuous kiai for multiple strikes of ten or more.

In reality, most kendoka try to achieve top speed and the end product is that feet move together in a jumping motion while the shoulders remain in the same place and the shinai swings wildly backwards and forwards without coming close to the intended target. To do choyaku suburi well, you need extensive practice. My only advice is that you should try to make it look more like the former description and less like the latter.

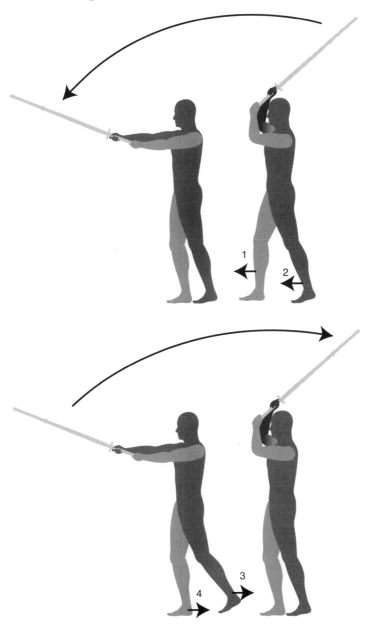

Sequences

All of the suburi described above are frequently practiced together at the beginning of the kendo session by all dojo members together. In this case the individual leading the suburi (often a senior student), calls out the exercises and sets the timing. Usually each form is repeated from 20 to 50 times. The list of suburi set out above could easily be practiced in that order starting with jogeburi and finishing with choyaku suburi.

Individual suburi practice

Suburi can of course be practiced without the benefit of other students or an instructor. If you have sufficient space, the routines described as well as far more complex "shadow sequences" can be attempted on your own. This approach can be used to work on the techniques themselves, or to put successive renzoku waza together and to explore seme, distance, and timing. If you are able to practice in front of a mirror it will help you correct mistakes.

You can also try some of the following:

- Kote men (men in one step, kote in one step, returning to your original position)

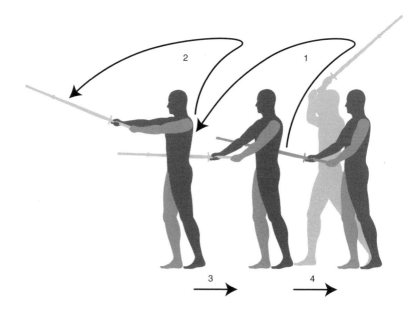

- Kote men dou (as above, either adding dou as a forward movement or a hiki waza)

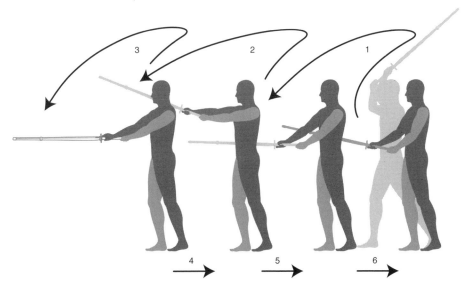

- Men gyaku dou.

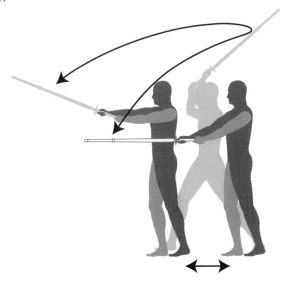

In essence, any technique or series of techniques can be practiced in suburi format. If you are practicing outside the dojo you may need to adapt your approach to cope with floor conditions and lack of headroom. (You can buy special suburi shinai that replicate the weight and feel of a shinai while being much shorter. You can also use your imagination and just your hands.)

Footwork drills

Footwork can also be practiced without a partner. In the dojo this normally takes the form of the instructor calling out the steps, or leading by example with the students following.

One exercise that is often used with kendoka in the early stages of training is to have them step forwards, backwards, left, and right in random patterns in okuri-ashi on the instructor's command. Usually instructions are given in Japanese – Mae, ato, migi, hidari. This is used to improve footwork, balance, and stability.

Variations of the following drill can also be employed to improve foot movement and coordination:

1. Students are lined up in ranks across the dojo ensuring that each has sufficient space around him or her. They then move along the length of the hall practicing okuri ashi footwork. The shinai can be placed horizontally behind the hips to ensure that posture is correct.

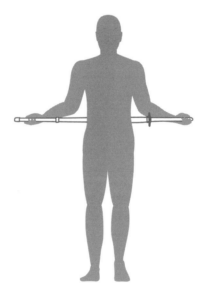

2. The next rank of students move forward as soon at the first rank is clear. On reaching the end of the dojo they return in the same way.

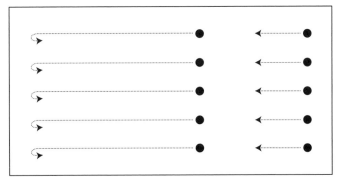

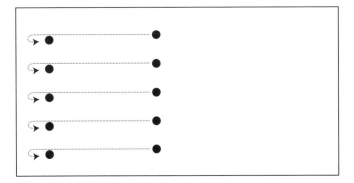

3. The exercise is repeated with the shinai held in chudan kamae.

4. One or two men strikes are then introduced on the instructor's command during each trip along the dojo's length.

5. Frequency of strike is then increased, for instance, step twice and strike on the third step.

6. Ni-dan waza such as kote men can also be introduced as can more complex renzoku waza sequences, both forwards and backwards.

Practicing With Children

Kendo can be practiced between people of different ages and sizes. Men and women train together; and it is possible for adults and children to do so. I recommend that this should be done only when the participating adults are sufficiently experienced to control the strength of their strikes and can stop forward movement at will. In this case a selected group of experienced adults should act as motodachi and the children as kakarite.

Once they have learned the basics, they should be able to practice with other children, ideally of similar age and size. Children's lessons should always be supervised by at least one qualified instructor and care should be taken to ensure that the practice is carried out safely.

Children can start kendo as young as six or seven, but should be taught in a way that they enjoy. Kendo should be seen as a way to let off steam and have fun. Very often this enjoyment distils itself into a desire to improve and continue growing as a kendoka.

Other Forms of Training

Seminars and gasshuku

Seminars

Seminars are regularly held before grading examinations or to concentrate on specific aspects of kendo such as refereeing. They can also give kendoka from various dojo the opportunity to get together to benefit from the teaching of visiting instructors.

Seminars can be aimed at a local, national, regional, or global level with FIK seminars for referees in the European, Asia Pacific, and Americas zones and the Gedatsukai summer camp which every year brings kendoka from around the World to Japan.

Kendo seminars can last for half a day up to 10 days and be attended on a daily basis or accommodation provided. Depending on the time available, seminars afford attendants the opportunity to look at elements of kendo in more detail than in normal keiko and also give them the chance to practice with new partners.

Gasshuku

Gasshuku are not dissimilar in purpose to seminars and can be for the benefit of members of a single dojo or open to wider groups. In essence gasshuku are training camps where kendoka spend a number of days living and training together in a communal environment. As well as working on kendo technique and stamina you learn to develop teamwork and to socialize with others.

Dojo visits

Kendoka who normally practice in small groups can benefit from the chance to train with other people afforded by dojo visits. These can be organized on a reciprocal basis with other dojo and may even include a friendly shiai.

Kangeiko and shochugeiko

These are training sessions held at the coldest (kangeiko) and hottest (shochugeiko) times of the year. These normally take the form of practices on consecutive days for a period of between one week and a month where kendoka concentrate on strenuous kihon geiko.

Hatsugeiko

Hatsugeiko is the first practice of the year. This is sometimes held to span midnight on New Year's Eve and referred to as toshikoshi geiko.

Asa geiko

Asa geiko is common in Japan, less so outside. Meaning morning practice this takes place at 6:00 or 7:00 A.M. and lasts for an hour.

Shiai

For some shiai or competition is the reason for practicing kendo. For others this is their least favorite aspect of the sport. Whatever your view, shiai is an integral element of kendo and gives the opportunity to test your skills in a "win or lose," "life or death" situation. Shiai is not the preserve of a small group of elite athletes, although these certainly exist within the context of The All Japan Championships. Within kendo people have the opportunity to compete throughout their lifetime; from junior competition to the Kyoto Taikai, where the final matches are played out by kenshi in their eighties.

Most country kendo organizations have regular regional and national competitions and there are annual championships for the main kendo zones. Once every three years, the Asia, Americas, and European zones take it in turns to host The World Kendo Championships.

There are no weight divisions in kendo but generally men's, women's, and junior competitions are held separately, often on the same day at the same venue. The match is held in a shiai-jo or court that may vary in size between 30 feet (9m) and 36 feet (11m) square. Depending on the size of the competition and the number of competitors, there could be up to eight shiai-jo in play at the same time. The court is marked with a center cross "chushin" and two lines from behind which competitors must start the competition.

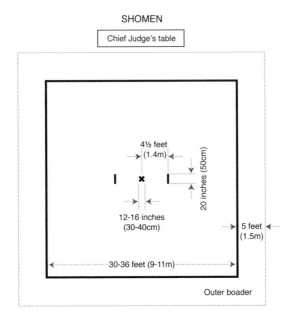

There are two main types of kendo shiai, individual and team. Kendo matches are based on a sanbon shobu (best of three points) scoring system and are judged by three referees who indicate with a red or white flag the techniques that they consider to have achieved a valid point or "yuko datotsu." To be judged as such, a point must be made "in high spirit" with the correct part of the shinai at the correct angle on the correct part of the kendo-gu. It must be made with clear intent and correct posture and be followed by zanshin (awareness and potential readiness to deal with a counterattack).

To score you need the agreement of two out of three referees, although if for any reason two did not see the point, the vote of one "shinpan" would make the point valid. In addition to points being awarded for valid attacks, penalty points are given for stepping out of the shiai area, for dropping the shinai, or touching the blade of one's own or the opponent's shinai and for a variety of other infringements that could be considered potentially dangerous or disrespectful.

Most competitions start with pool rounds, so that players have the chance to fight with at least two opponents before elimination or progression through a series of tournament rounds. The time for each bout is set at five minutes, although the organizers are free to make it shorter. In the event of no point being scored an open ended extension or encho is called and the match decided by one point. In cases when an encho fails to deliver a score, referees are able to decide an outcome by hantei or vote. This is usually awarded to the fighter with the stronger technique and fighting spirit.

Although there are numerous exceptions, team matches are usually for teams of five fighters who are allocated set positions in the fighting order. From first to last these are senpo, jiho, chuken, fukusho, and taisho. A team manager or coach will select people for these positions on their skills and temperaments, so a quick starter is ideal as senpo and typically the strongest player is chosen as taisho.

As in all aspects of kendo, reigi, or etiquette, is important in shiai. At the beginning of the first shiai and at the end of the last shiai of each competition all referees and competitors will bow to shomen (the high place in the hall). Competitors start and finish each match by bowing to each other.

For individual competitions, players will step in to the shiai-jo bow and take three steps to the staring position and assume sonkyo before the main referee's instruction of hajime to start. They will finish on the instruction yame and reverse the process. In the case of team competitions the teams will line up facing each other inside the shiai jo with senpo closest to the main referee.

Beginning of the first match

SHOMEN

Chief Judge's table

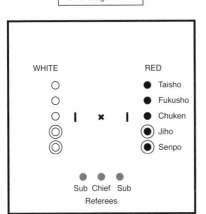

WHITE ○ ○ ○ ◎ ◎ | × | ● Taisho ● Fukusho ● Chuken ⦿ Jiho ⦿ Senpo   RED

Sub Chief Sub
Referees

The end of the match

SHOMEN

Chief Judge's table

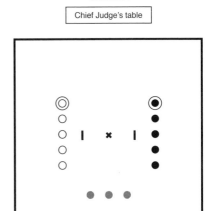

◎ ○ ○ ○ ○ | × | ⦿ ● ● ● ●

◎ ⦿ competitors wear men and kote and carry shinai

He and jiho only should wear men and kote and carry shinai. At the end of the match the fighters return to the same position with only Taisho armed.

Fighters face each other individually with matches scored on the best of three system. Results are decided on the number of individual wins and draws. If even the points are counted and in the event of a stalemate, a representative is chosen from each team for a one point "daihyo" match.

Other forms of team match also exist. The Red and White, kachinuki system used in the Tozai Taikai lets the winner stay on until he is eventually defeated. The Todofuken (inter-prefectural) Taikai in Japan now consists of teams of seven athletes drawn from different sections of the kendo community. Formerly teams for this numbered nine with two female competitors included. There is now a separate ladies competition.

It is essential that shiai competitors work towards developing a "level mind," that continues to flow under pressure. Only regular and intense keiko will give you the ability to react to opportunities in shiai as if by second nature. I believe that for shiai to become a valuable part of the kendo learning experience, you need to be ready for it. It is counterproductive to start your shiai career before you have developed correct basic movement. Some competitions for children now consist of a demonstration of kirikaeshi or basic technique demonstration or keiko which is judged on hantei.

Refereeing Kendo Matches

As described in the shiai section, kendo matches are refereed by three "shinpan" who are responsible for judging accurate yuko-datotsu and for facilitating the smooth and safe running of the shiai. These referees are positioned

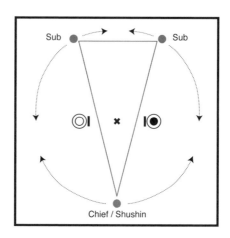

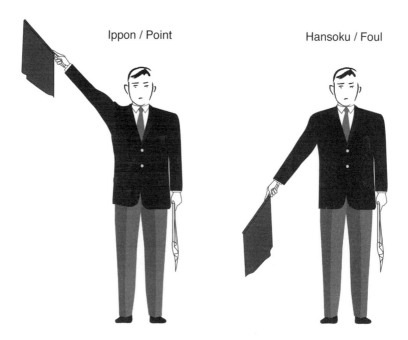

Ippon / Point

Hansoku / Foul

in a triangle around the two competitors so that they can see each other's signals while keeping both players in full view. Yuko datotsu and infringements are signalled with red or white flags, which match the "mejirushi" or "tasuki" ribbons attached to each player.

The referee at the point of the triangle is known as shushin and he or she is responsible for making all commands and announcements to the shiai competitors. The other two referees or fukushin have equal responsibility with shushin but do not issue commands. Normally referees change position after an agreed number of matches and alternate in the shushin role.

Unlike in some sports, becoming a referee is an integral part of one's kendo development. From third dan upwards, kendoka are expected to take their place as referees in parallel with their own keiko and shiai commitments. It is mandatory that referees be active kendoka and kendo referees are viewed as colleagues rather than outsiders.

Becoming a skilled referee takes a lot of practice and understanding of the rules and refereeing theory. To that end, the International Kendo Federation run regular referees seminars in the main kendo zones and these are then replicated by the member country organisations.

Referees for international events are selected on their ability and track record as a referee and not just by kendo seniority. It is however unlikely that referees at major international competitions will be below the grade of 6th or 7th dan. Generally it is difficult for referees to accurately judge the technique of players who are at a higher level than themselves.

The mindset of a kendo referee should not differ from that of a competitor. The challenge is to follow the shiai with an open mind that is not distracted from the main task of judging yuko datotsu. The biggest challenges that a referee faces are around issues of multitasking. For instance, when a competitor is close to the shiai-jo boundary line, referees are drawn to focus on his or her feet to see whether a foot crosses the line and earns a jogai hansoku. Unfortunately by concentrating on this one potential issue, there is a chance that eyes are looking down when ippon is scored and the point is missed.

There are numerous situations like this that can affect referees, particularly shushin who has responsibility for listening for the time signal, watching the scoreboard, and remembering the correct senkoku commands. It is all too easy to get caught up in procedural issues, constantly stopping a shiai because contestants are in tsubazeriai, or shinai are twisted, or equipment needs adjusting. In reality the key function of the shinpan is to facilitate the smooth running of the shiai, while accurately judging yuko datotsu.

Refereeing is an intrinsic part of our kendo development and should be regarded as any other aspect of our keiko. Not seeing the whole picture means we are looking too narrowly at one element of a match in the same way that we are unlikely to successfully strike men or kote if we look only at the target. Both shiaisha and referees should be using "enzan no metsuke."

The problem of fixation on one element of a match can be described as shishin or stopped mind, which is the opposite condition to hoshin, the condition that lets your mind wander freely through the flow of the shiai whether you are a fighter or a referee.

Like keiko, refereeing can be frustrating and painful, but in the same way when you achieve a breakthrough it is very satisfying and lessons learned in keiko build your ability as a referee and vice versa.

Grading Examinations

Kendo has a rigid, objective system for grading examinations which is enforced all the way up the ladder to 8th dan. The method of examination is by appraisal by a panel of senior kendoka. Their numbers and grades are regulated against the grade being taken. Typically examiners must hold a minimum grade of 3rd dan and be two dan grades higher than the candidates who are being examined.

Panels range from three in number for 1st kyu to five for 1st to 3rd dan with six panelists required for 4th to 7th dan. In the case of 8th dan there are two sessions with a preliminary test examined by a panel of seven senior 8th dans increasing to fourteen for the second examination.

As mentioned before, kyu grades up to 2nd kyu are awarded at club level, 1st kyu to 5th dan is a national (or in Japan, prefectural) grade, and in most geographies 6th dan upwards is under the control of the International Kendo Federation or The All Japan Kendo Federation. While there are slight variations between countries and for different grades, examinations typically consist of two parts: Jitsugi (exhibition jigeiko) with two partners and for candidates who are successful at this stage, an examination of kendo no kata. In some countries the jitsugi portion includes a demonstration of kirikaeshi for candidates up to 3rd dan. A written theory examination can also be part of the process.

The aim wherever possible, is for candidates to be unknown to judges to ensure impartiality. Zekken are removed and replaced with a grading number and in some cases overly large names on hakama or keikogi are taped over.

Attitude in grading examinations is exceptionally important. Candidates are there to demonstrate the skills that they have developed since their last grading, so need to adopt a confident open manner where they can create opportunities to show their qualities. It is easy to mistakenly assume that grading jitsugi is the same as shiai and that your objective is to beat your opponent. This is not the case. Theoretically, even at the highest level of 8th dan it is possible for two opponents to pass together although at this level the pass rate is so low that it rarely happens.

The real objective is to show the panel the skills that are required to pass a particular grade. This cannot be done if grading partners are defensive and afraid of losing points. Rather than worrying about being hit, they should concentrate on making their own effective attacks and counterattacks.

To prepare for grading examinations, kendoka should first understand what qualities the examiners will be looking for and to work on those points in their regular dojo practice. A good instructor will typically be aware of what you need to work on and encourage you to carry out the right kind of training so that you build on your kendo with the aim of bringing the required elements together at examination time. Occasionally the kindest thing he or she might tell you is to keep training and be patient until the next opportunity. Sometimes tackling a grading before you are ready may do more harm than good.

It is worth keeping in mind that it normally takes months not weeks or days to make sustainable changes to your kendo, so while a grading seminar may be offered just before the examination date, its only real benefits are to remind you of what you already know and to help make you familiar with the procedures that will take place on the day.

The day before your grading you should try to rest and take your mind off the event. You should be careful to eat well without overeating or consuming too much alcohol. On the day itself you should aim to keep calm, confident, and enthusiastic so that you can display your technique and spirit to the full. Every kendo keiko, shiai, and grading examination is unpredictable for the same reason it is interesting. The outcome evolves from the way in which two individuals react to each other. So While you may have prepared to the pitch of perfection, the luck of the draw may dictate that you may get an opponent who makes it difficult for you to look your best. Typically it is better to grade against a technically strong opponent that a weak, overly defensive one. If the worst happens, there is always next time.

Remember the panel can only judge you on what they see. In 99 percent of cases they hope to see you deliver the evidence they need to pass you. To impress the examination panel, from the moment you stand up from sonkyo, your posture and balance needs to show that you are able to move as soon as the opportunity arises. Your initial kiai should be loud and intense and you should also show restraint when there is no obvious chance to attack. Most importantly, you need to be able to step into your opponents distance, take the initiative and instantly hit men or kote. Two or three ippon with each opponent is enough, although you will not be penalized for making more successful strikes. You stand most chance of success if you can remain relaxed and flexible.

The jitsugi section of the examination is conducted in a pool system with candidate A fighting candidate B, candidate B going on to a second bout with candidate C who then faces candidate D with candidate A then returning to take on candidate D. In that way everyone faces two opponents.

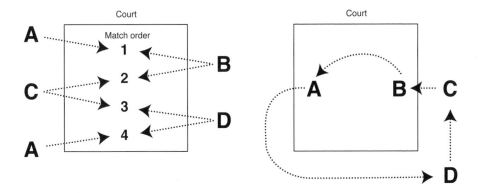

Those that pass the jitsugi section are required to take a kata examination. The number of kata performed depends on the dan grade being examined. In this section the number of required kata need to be performed without error. In the case of a mistake, the head judge will give the candidate one more chance to repeat the action correctly. If he or she repeats the error they are considered to have failed the kata section of the grading and must re-apply for the next examination. Most kendo federations will allow candidates to retry just the kata section without having to go through the whole process.

Glossary/Index

AJKF   All Japan Kendo Federation. See page 9.
Aruki-ashi   See ayumi-ashi. See page 92.
Asa geiko   Morning practice. See page 174.
Aun-kokyu   Breathing in through the nose out through the mouth. Used in meditation forms. See page 44.
Ayumi-ashi   Walking footwork. See pages 42, 123, 138, and 147.
Bogu   Kendo Armor. See pages 12, 17, 18, 33, 147, and 150.
Bokuto   Wooden sword used for kata. Also called boken. See page 147.
Bu/rin   Old measures used to measure the distance of kendo hand stitching. See page 18.
Butsukarigeiko   Taiatari practice. See pages 110 and 111.
Chakuza   Alternative command to seiza for sit in formal position. See page 32.
Chichikawa   Leather loop through which himo is tied. See page18.
Chigiri   Metal plate inside shinai handle. See page 22.
Chikai maai   Close distance. See pages 39 and 115.
Choyaku suburi   Jumping suburi. See pages 166, 167, and 168.
Chudan kamae   Center kamae. See pages 34, 36, 53, 55, 59, 61, 96, 129, 140, 141, 163, 164, 166, and 171.
Chuken   Middle fighter in a team match. See pages 176 and 177.
Chushin   Center. See page 175.
Daimyo   Feudal lord. See page 27.
Daito   Long sword. See page 23.
Dan-ii   Dan grade system. See page 29.
Datotsu bu   striking area of shinai (one quarter of the total shinai length measured from kisaki). See pages 49, 77, 113, and 135.
Datotsu-bui   valid target areas. See page 41.
Debana waza   Attack as opponent begins his attack. See pages 64, 65, and 80.
Degote   Strike to kote as your opponent starts to attack. See page 66.
Dobari   Shinai shape with a bulge toward the tsuba end. See page 24.
Dogi   Clothing worn for martial arts training. See page 10.

Dojo	A place in which a martial art is practiced. See pages 7, 8, 12, 19, 27, 28, 29, 32, 33, 44, 106, 145, 153, 160, 161, 170, 171, and 173.
Dou	Kendo trunk protector and strike to the body. See pages 12, 17, 18, 19, 35, 41, 48, 51, 59, 60, 61, 72, 73, 79, 86, 92, 98, 103, 106, 108, 118, 122, 123, 131, 133, 135, 136, 137, 138, 166, and 169.
Dou dai	Dou plate. See pages 17 and 48.
Dou mune	Top of the dou. See page 130.
Dou uchi	Strike to dou. See pages 59, 106, and 118.
Enzan no metsuke	"Looking at a mountain," a way of looking at the whole picture in kendo. See pages 45, 46, and 180.
FIK	International Kendo Federation. See pages 23, 29, and 173.
Fudō Myō-ō	Buddhist "King of Wisdom". See page 11.
Fudoshin	Immovable mind. See page 11.
Fukushin	Subsidiary referee. See page 179.
Fukusho	Fourth fighter in a team match. See pages 176 and 177.
Fumikomi-ashi	Stamping footwork. See pages 42 and 43.
Furikaburi	To swing upwards. See page 136.
Futon	Cushion - The parts of kendo armor made to absorb blows. See pages 8 and 21.
Gan	Sight. See page 45.
Gasshuku	Training camp. See page 173
Gedan kamae	Guard posture where the shinai is pointed down at a 45 degree angle. See page 39.
Gojo	The five Confucian virtues - Humanity, Justice, Courtesy, Wisdom and Faith (Jin-Gi-Rei-chi-shin). See page 13.
Gokakugeiko	Free practice between players of equal level. See pages 143, 144, and 145.
Gyaku-dou	Reverse dou, left dou. See pages 48 and 61.
Hajime	Command to begin. See page 176.
Hakama	Divided skirt worn in kendo. See pages 12, 13, 14, 15, 18, and 181.
Hanshi	The highest character / teaching rank in kendo. See page 29.
Hansoku	Penalty in kendo shiai. See pages 77 and 178.
Harai waza	Make opportunity by sweeping the shinai aside. See pages 64, 69, 72, and 124.
Hasso kamae	Guard posture where the shinai is held on the right shoulder. See page 38.
Hasuji	The path (angle) of the blade. See pages 49, 61, 106, 118, and 135.
Hatsugeiko	First practice of the year. See page 174.
Hayasuburi	Jumping suburi. See page 166.
Hidari	Left. See page 170.
Hidari-kote	Left kote. See page 48.
Hikibana waza	Attack as opponent retreats. See page 64.
Hiki-giri	A strike where the shinai is pulled backwards. See page 61.

Hikitategeiko	Free practice between instructor and pupil. See pages 111, 144, 145, 146, and 152.
Hikitsuke	Drawing the left foot up so that toes are in line with the right heel. See pages 62, 118, 126, and 130.
Hiki-waza	Technique made whilst stepping backwards. See page 61.
Himo	Cords used to fasten bogu. See pages 18 and 21.
Hiraki-ashi	Diagonal footwork. See page 43.
Hitori Geiko	Individual practice. See pages 8 and 161.
Ippon	Point in kendo. See pages 178, 179, and 182.
Ippon Shobu	One point match. See page 146.
Issoku ito maai	One step, one cut distance. See pages 66, 108, 114, 116, 136, 138, and 147.
Jigeiko	Free practice. See pages 64, 101, 102, 143, 144, 145, 146, 151, 152, and 181.
Jiho	Second fighter in a team match. See pages 176 and 177.
Jinbu	The blade (cutting part) of the shinai. See pages 24, 73, and 77.
Jitsugi	The keiko section of a grading examination. See pages 181, 182, and 183.
Jodan kamae	Guard posture where the shinai is held above the head. See pages 39 and 161.
Jogai	Stepping out of shiai-jo boundary. See page 179.
Jogeburi	Swinging shinai in a big arc. See page 168.
Joseki	The high end of the dojo sometimes referred to as shomen. See pages 28 and 32.
Kachinuki	"Winner fights again" shiai format. See page 177.
Kaeshi-waza	Return technique, blocking on one side of the shinai and returning the technique on the other. See page 43.
Kakarigeiko	Continuous attacking practice. See pages 103, 104, 110, 111, 144, 146, 151, and 152.
Kakarite	Attacker. See pages 66, 82, 92, 98, 103, 104, 107, 108, 109, 110, 111, 124, 125, 126, 127, 129, 130, 131, 133, 139, 140, 141, 144, 145, 146, and 172.
Kakegoe	Kendo shout. See pages 45 and 107.
Kamae	Guard posture. See pages 31, 34, 37, 39, 41, 49, 63, 64, 69, 70, 71, 77, 80, 91, 94, 96, 110, 143, and 144.
Kamidana	Small shinto shrine found in many Japanese dojo. See page 27.
Kamiza	As Joseki. See pages 27, 28, and 145.
Kangeiko	Winter practice. See page 173.
Kansai himo	Long men himo tied from the top of the men to the tsukidate and back to the top. Formerly popular in Western Japan. See page 21.
Kanto himo	Shorter himo tied from the bottom of the men upwards. See page 21.

Kata	A pre-arranged series of techniques practiced without bogu. See pages 147, 151, and 183.
Kata geiko	Kata training. See pages 147 and 151.
Katana	Japanese sword. See pages 9, 24, 31.
Katatetsuki	Single handed tsuki. See pages 62 and 63.
Keiko	Generic term for kendo training has the connotation of "reflecting on the past." See pages 10, 18, 24, 28, 29, 30, 31, 59, 106, 111, 143, 144, 145, 146, 152, 173, 177, 179, 180, and 182.
Keikogi	Kendo jacket. See pages 12, 13, 15, 17, and 181.
Kendo	"The way of the sword." See pages 7, 8, 9, 11, 12, 27, 28, 51, 143, 147, 151, 172, and 181.
kendo-gu	See bogu.
Kendoka	Kendo player. See pages 7, 8, 11, 24, 27, 34, 44, 101, 104, 152, 172, 123, 179, and 182.
Kendo-no-kata	Fixed kendo forms practiced without armor. See page 150.
Kenshi	Kendo player. See pages 80 and 175.
Ki	Spirit / energy. See page 80.
Kiai	Literally meeting each other's energy, commonly used to mean the kendo shout. See pages 44, 45, 106, 107, 115, 143, 161, 166, and 182.
Kigurai	Pride / Commanding presence. See page 34.
Kihaku	Strength of spirit. See pages 9, 10, 55, and 82.
Kihon geiko	Basic practice. See pages 101, 102, 143, and 173.
Ki-ken-tai-itchi	The unity of mind, sword and body. See page 106.
Kirikaeshi	Series of connected shomen and yoko men strikes for training. See pages 45, 102, 103, 105, 106, 138, 146, 151, 152, 165, 177, and 181.
Kisaki	Sword point. See pages 26 and 66.
Kizeme	Seme based on the strength of the attackers spirit. See page 80.
Koban	Oval handled shinai (shaped like old Japanese coin). See page 24.
Kobushi	The fist part of the kote. See page 24.
Kodachi-no-kata	Short sword kata. See page 23.
Kodansha	Senior dan grade. See page 29.
Kohai	Junior. See page 27.
Kokoro	Heart, mind. See page 31.
Kokyu	Breathing. See page 31.
Koshi-ita	The rigid part at the back of a hakama. See page 15.
Kote	Kendo glove also the wrist as a target or a strike to the wrist. See pages 8, 12, 18, 19, 21, 32, 33, 41, 49, 51, 54, 56, 57, 58, 60, 66, 67, 69, 71, 73, 76, 77, 84, 85, 90, 91, 96, 108, 109, 115, 116, 117, 118, 168, 177, 180, and 182.
Kote-uchi	Strike to kote. See page 56.
Koto	(old style) Straight shaped shinai. See page 24.

Kyoshi	The 2nd level of the three shogo grades, now reserved for 7th dan and above. See page 29.
Kyoto Taikai	Annual kendo festival held in Kyoto. See pages 175 and 191.
Kyu	Grades awarded by the dojo before a kendoka graduates into the Dan ranks. See pages 28 and 181.
Kyudan	9th Dan (No longer awarded). See page 28.
Maai	Distance. See pages 39 and 42.
Madake	Literally timber bamboo. In kendo this term normally refers to expensive hand-made shinai. See page 25.
Makiage	Knocking the shinai up in a wrapping motion. See page 64.
Makiotoshi	Knocking the shinai down in a wrapping motion. See pages 64.
Makoto	Sincerity. See page 13.
Mawari geiko	Practice format where partners change at the end of each exercise on command. See pages 102, 103, 112, 145, and 152.
Mejirushi	Red or white ribbons used to differentiate fighters in shiai. See page 179.
Men	Face mask, the head as a target, and a strike to the head. See pages 12, 18, 19, 21, 32, 36, 37, 41, 45, 47, 49, 51, 55, 59, 66, 69, 73, 105, 109, 171, 177, 181, and 182.
Men wo torre	Command to take off men. See page 32.
Men wo tsuke	Command to put on men. See pages 19 and 32.
Men-uchi	Strike to men. See pages 53 and 115.
Mengane	The bars of the face mask. See page 106.
Metsuke	Vision in kendo (see Enzan no metsuke)
Migi	Right. See page 170.
Migi-kote	Right kote. See page 47.
Mitsu no sen	The three timings Sen, Sen no Sen, and Go no sen. See page 51.
Mokuso	Brief meditation before keiko. See pages 30, 32, and 44.
Morotetsuki	Two handed tsuki. See page 62.
Motodachi	Receiver. See pages 66, 82, 84, 85, 86, 87, 90, 92, 98, 99, 103, 104, 106, 107, 108, 109, 110, 111, 117, 124, 125, 129, 131, 138, 141, 144, 145, 146, 152, and 172.
Motodachi geiko	Practice where the senior grade takes a teaching role. See page 102.
Mukaetsuki	Thrust as opponent steps forward, potentially dangerous and considered bad manners. See page 63.
Munehimo	Top tie on the keikogi. See page 13.
Mushin	"No mind" - A state where you can produce technique without thinking. See pages 7 and 66.
Nafuda	See Zekken
Nakayui	Leather strip tied around the shinai at approximately a third the length of the jinbu from the tip. See pages 22, 26, and 49.
Naname buri	Diagonal suburi. See page 163.

Nayashi	The technique of pushing your hands forward to deflect tsuki while stepping back. See page 99.
Nito	Style of kendo using two swords. See page 23.
Nodo	The throat, target for tsuki. See page 34.
Nuki-Waza	Avoiding technique, move the target away from your opponents strike while responding with your own attack. See page 43.
Oji waza	Counter attack. See pages 41, 51, 59, 80, 81, 82, 100, 103, 104, 110, 124, 135, 144, and 145.
Okuri-ashi	Footwork where left foot is drawn up to right heel. See pages 42 and 170.
Omote	The inner side of the sword. See pages 69, 70, 73, 88, 92, and 170.
Osae	Push down or against the shinai. See pages 71 and 110.
Reigi	Courtesy. See pages 19, 27, and 176.
Reigi saho	Method of showing courtesy. See page 27.
Reiho	Method of showing courtesy. See pages 27, 32, and 33.
Renshi	The most junior of the shogo grades 6th dan and above is eligible. See page 29.
Renzoku waza	Continuous attacks. See pages 64, 73, 168, and 171.
Riki	Power, strength. See pages 46.
Sakigawa	Leather cap at the end of the shinai. See pages 22, 23, and 25.
Sakigomu	Rubber stopper inside shinai cap. See page 22.
Sansappo	Three ways of beating the opponent (sometimes called san satsu ho). See page 81.
Sanbon shobu	Best of three points. See page 176.
Seiretsu	Command to line up. See page 32.
Seiza	Sitting with legs folded with the buttocks between the feet. Can also be used instead of Mokuso. See pages 18, 29, 30, and 32.
Seme	To break through your opponents center (literally attack). See pages 42, 64, 66, 70, 80, 81, 101, 103, 114, 115, 124, 145, and 168.
Sempai	Senior. See pages 23 and 33.
Senpo	First fighter in a team match. See pages 176 and 177.
Sensei	A term of respect for teachers (literally "born before"). See pages 7, 10, 27, 32, 33, 36, and 145.
Shaku/sun	Old measures used to measure the length of shinai. See page 23
Shiai	Kendo contest. See pages 39, 59, 73, 173, 175, 176, 177, 178, 179, 180, 181, and 182.
Shiai-jo	Competition area between 30 and 36 feet square (9 and 11 meters square). See pages 175, 176, and 179.
Shidachi	The junior partner in Kendo-no-kata. See pages 147, 148, and 150.
Shihan	Dojo Master, Chief instructor. See page 12.
Shi kai	4 sicknesses of kendo. See page 80.
Shikake waza	Attacking technique. See pages 51, 52, 56, 64, 76, 80, 81, 100, 124, 144, and 145.

Shimoza	Student side of the dojo. See pages 27, 28, and 145.
Shinai	Bamboo practice sword. See pages12, 22, 23, 24, 25, 26, 31, 33, 35, 36, 37, 38, 46, 49, 55, 73, 150, 161, 162, 163, 164, 165, 170, 176, 177, and 179.
Shinogi	The "shoulder" of the blade. See page 88.
Shinpan	Referee. See pages 176, 178, and 179.
Shinzen	Sometimes used to refer to high side of dojo. See page 28.
Shisei	Posture. See page 31.
Shochugeiko	Summer practice. See page 173
Shodachi	First point of a shiai or jigeiko. See pages 143, 144, and 146.
Shogo	The three teaching/character grades of Renshi, Kyoshi, Hanshi. See page 29.
Shomen	Used as a less formal reference for joseki and kamiza or can mean a straight strike to the men. See pages 27, 28, 29, 32, 45, 82, 106, 107, 175, 176, and 177.
Shomen suburi	Suburi to men height. See pages 163, 164, and 166.
Shoto	Short sword used in Ni-to. See page 23.
Shudokan	Osaka Castle dojo. See page 28.
Shushin	Main referee. See pages 178 and 179.
Soku	Foot/speed. See page 45.
Sonkyo	Squatting salutation at the beginning and end of keiko. See pages 31, 143, 176, and 182.
Suburi	Repeated practice swings. See pages 44, 151, 161, 168, and 169.
Suriage waza	Sliding up technique used to move opponent's shinai off course before striking. See page 82.
Suri-ashi	Sliding footwork. See page 42.
Sutemi	Sacrifice. Committing 100 percent to an attack. Literally "throw away the seeds." See page 52.
Tabi	Japanese traditional socks. See page 44.
Tachi-no-kata	Long sword kata. See pages 147 and 150.
Tai sabaki	Body movement, moving your body to avoid or strike opponent. See page 110.
Taiatari	Body check after striking. See pages 76, 105, 110, and 111.
Taisho	Captain in a team match. See pages 176 and 177.
Take	Bamboo. See pages 22, 24, 25, 26, and 49.
Tame	The condition of holding yourself in readiness to attack. See pages 66 and 80.
Tan	Abdomen (courage). See page 46.
Tanden	Abdomen (courage). See page 44.
Tare	Apron to protect the hips and groin. See pages 12, 18, and 19.
Tasuki	See Mejirushi.
Tenouchi	Grip on completing a strike, literally "inside of the hand". See pages 24, 37, 58, 112, 161, and 164

Tenugui	Cotton towel worn under men. See pages 12, 19, 20, and 21.
Tobikomi waza	Attack in your own timing. See page 64.
Todofuken Taikai	Inter City, Prefectural match held annually in Japan. See page 177.
Toi maai	Long distance. See pages 39, 109, 114, and 117.
Toshikoshi geiko	New Year's Eve practice. See page 174.
Tozai Taikai	East, West Match. See page 177.
Tsuba	Sword guard. See pages 24, 31, 36, and 77.
Tsubazeriai	Close position where fighters are "tsuba to tsuba." See pages 58, 64, 76, 77, and 179.
Tsugi-ashi	Bringing the left foot up level or almost level with the right foot before making an attack. See page 42.
Tsuka	Shinai handle. See pages 24 and 35.
Tsukagawa	Leather cover on shinai handle. See pages 22, 24, 25, and 26.
Tsuki	Thrust to the throat. See pages 47, 51, 62, 63, 73, 76, 89, and 179.
Tsuru	String on top edge of shinai. See pages 22, 25, and 26.
Tsutsu	Flexible part of kote at wrist joint. See page 18.
Uchidachi	The senior partner in Kendo-no-kata. See pages 147, 148, and 150.
Uchikomi geiko	Striking practice. See pages 102, 103, 108, 109, 111, 144, 151, and 152.
Uchikomi-bo	Stick used by instructor to receive strikes. See page 109.
Uchima	Your "own" distance. See pages 41 and 66.
Uchiotoshi waza	Technique used to make an opportunity by knocking the opponents shinai down See pages 64 and 82.
Ura	The outer side of the sword. See pages 69, 70, and 88.
Waki gamae	Guard posture where the shinai is held behind the right side of the body. See page 38.
Waza	Technique. See pages 45, 51, 80, 81, 112, 124, 143, and 144.
Waza geiko	Technique practice. See pages 103, 111, 112, 151, and 152.
Yakusoku geiko	Practice of pre-arranged techniques. See pages 109 and 111.
Yame	Command to stop. See page 176.
Yoko-men	Diagonal cut to the temple. See pages 47, 105, 106, and 107.
Yotsuware shinai	Shinai made of four bamboo slats. See page 22.
Yuko-datotsu	Valid strikes. See pages 46, 58, and 178.
Zanshin	Awareness of opponent on completion of attack. See pages 45, 49, 55, 58, 61, 68, 77, 105, 124, and 176.
Zazen	Zen meditation. See page 30.
Zekken	Covers worn on central flap of tare bearing players name and dojo. See page 181.
Zenshin kotai shomen suburi	Continuous shomen suburi. See pages 164 and 165.
ZNKR	Zen Nippon Kendo Renmei (AJKF). See page 152.

The Author

Geoff Salmon holds the grade of 7th Dan and is one of the few westerners to have passed the new All Japan Kendo Federation kyoshi examination.

Geoff teaches kendo in the UK and throughout Europe. He has held a number of key kendo posts including that of Chairman of the British Kendo Association and Manager of the British National Kendo Squad. He was a director of the 12th World Kendo Championship in Scotland where he had the honor of welcoming Her Majesty Queen Elizabeth and HRH the Duke of Edinburgh.

Geoff is familiar with high-level kendo competition as a competitor and referee, with four recent appearances at the Kyoto Taikai to add to his record of earlier competition in the European and World Championships. He has refereed at The European Championships on numerous occasions and was selected as a referee for the 15th World Kendo Championships, 2012. Geoff is an active blogger and writes regularly on kendo technique and culture at www.kendoinfo.net.

He spent three years living and training in Japan, spreading his time between Osaka Shudokan and several dojo in Hyogo. He was fortunate enough to study directly with some of the great 2nd generation kendo teachers including Matsumoto Toshio, Hanshi 9th dan. He still visits Japan as often as possible to further his own training.

In his spare time he is a partner in a headhunting firm and lives in Surrey in the UK.

The Illustrator

Katsuya Masagaki holds 5th dan in kendo and a Master's degree in Graphic Design from Central St. Martin's College of Art and Design. Before moving to London in 1992 he worked as an art director and designer at a major advertising agency in Japan. He recently moved back to his native Kobe where he runs his own design consultancy www.katsuya.co.uk. He has worked on a number of kendo related projects including the design theme for the 12th World Kendo Championships in Glasgow, Scotland in 2003.